A TIME OF WAITING

In Memory of my mother Nuala Meldon
who died on the Feast of the Annunciation
March 25 2000

Anne Thurston

A Time of Waiting

IMAGES AND INSIGHTS

the columba press

First published in 2004 by
the columba press
55A Spruce Avenue, Stillorgan Industrial Park,
Blackrock, Co Dublin

Cover by Bill Bolger
Origination by The Columba Press
Printed in Ireland by ColourBooks Ltd, Dublin

ISBN 1 85607 471 4

Acknowledgements

The author wishes to thank a most courteous proof-reader who is, however, not responsible for any remaining errors! Thanks are due also to a
constant companion on journeys near and far. Finally, my gratitude
goes to a publisher willing to risk this Advent adventure into art and
text.

The author and publisher gratefully acknowledge the permission of
the following to quote from copyright material: Kathleen Norris for her
poem 'Advent'; Macmillan Publishers Ltd for Charles Causley's 'Ballad
of the Breadman'; Carcanet Press Ltd for Elizabeth Jennings' 'The
Visitation'; Bloodaxe Books Ltd for poems by Denise Levertov.

The lines from 'The Spirit of Place', copyright © 2002, 1981 by
Adrienne Rich; the line from 'Integrity' copyright © 2002, 1981 by
Adrienne Rich; the lines from 'Prospective Immigrants Please Note'
copyright 2002, 1967, 1963 by Adrienne Rich, from *The Fact of a
Doorframe: Selected Poems 1950-2001* by Adrienne Rich. Used by permis-
sion of the author and W. W. Norton & Co Inc.

Our thanks also to Patrick Mung Mung for the use of his father's
carving of 'Mary of Warmun'. The other three pictures were reproduced from transparencies supplied by The Bridgeman Art Library.

Contents

Illustrations

Introduction

Advent and Beyond

Advent is a very short liturgical season and it has become increasingly difficult to register it as anything other than a pre-Christmas period. I am interested in looking at Advent as a time which evokes a longing and an expectancy which reaches far beyond the celebration of Christmas. Its symbols of darkness and light are perennially powerful as are its themes of memory and hope.

As our world has become ever more fragile, with the growing threat of terrorist attacks, with eruptions of violence and ecological disasters, we have become dulled by apathy and numbed by fear. The readings for the first Sundays of Advent seem surprisingly relevant. Luke talks of 'nation rising against nation and kingdom against kingdom; earthquakes and famines ... people dying of fear as they await what menaces the world.' We are alerted to the need to 'Watch ... to stay awake.' And at the same time we are offered words of consolation and promise: 'In those days and at that time I will make a virtuous branch grow for David, who shall practise honesty and integrity in the land'. The choice is, as always, between fear and trust.

To enter into the space of stillness offered by the season of Advent is not to escape from the world but to come to see it more clearly. Everything around us conspires against the possibility of allowing us to walk in darkness and yet this is what we must do before we can come to the light. The longest night leads to the sweetest dawn. In a similar way our culture resists silence, refuses us a space of stillness, but this is also what we need before we can receive Wisdom's word. The poet Patrick Kavanagh

speaks of the 'Advent-darkened room' which can restore the soul
to wonder.[1] The Dominican, Timothy Radcliffe quotes Pascal:

> I have discovered that the unhappiness of human beings
> comes from just one thing; not knowing how to remain quietly
> in a room.[2]

Radcliffe insists on the importance of silence so that we may be
ready to be surprised by the gifts of knowledge or insight. Only
in silence can we be nudged by grace.

Advent offers a space of stillness, a time of darkness, a place
of waiting in expectant trust. The liturgies of Advent do not
cloak our fears but unmask them so that we may face the shadows and yet proclaim our hope.

From Darkness to Light

I have always looked forward to Advent. I spent time in
Germany as a student and in a way discovered the season there.
The homes I visited displayed their Advent wreaths and even if,
for some, they had lost their religious significance the residual
memory of evergreen hope remained, together with the ever
potent wonder of candlelight. We introduced this practice with
our own children and the making of the wreath and the lighting
of the candles on each successive Sunday has always been an
important ritual. My introduction to the Anglican Cathedral
tradition of the Advent procession added yet another rich dimension. On the first Sunday of Advent the congregation gathers
in a darkened church on a midwinter afternoon. They listen to
the readings from Isaiah prophesying the shining of a great light
on a people who sit in darkness. This becomes a present reality
as the people sit in the expectant dark and wait for the light to
come. As they are stilled, voices sound from far off singing the
Advent prose: 'Rorate coeli', 'Drop down ye heavens from
above and let the skies pour forth righteousness.' The flickering
candles are carried as the procession moves slowly through the
building while the words and music tell the story of humanity's
hope for salvation. These texts which express the yearning of
generations for the birth of a Messiah also evoke our own needs
and longing now.

The effect of this service is profound because we experience bodily what is being proclaimed. Even the simple matter of waiting for the choir to reach us, for our little candle to be lit, is a physical reminder of 'Advent waiting'. The symbols speak.

There is a symbolic procession from west to east as the choir and clergy move from the very back of the church towards the altar, stopping along the way for readings and carols.

Of course, as in all rituals which have richness and depth, there is an ambiguity here, as this is not simply a recollection of a past event but a calling forth in the present, bringing us to reflect now not just on birth, but also on death and judgement, on heaven and hell, on darkness and light, on wilderness and hope, on desolation and joy.

Advent is ever more counter-cultural. A few paces from these cathedrals where people sit and wait in the darkness, the alternative cathedrals of the shopping centres shine their bright and relentless lights and blare out Christmas carols, already stale, and it is only the beginning of December. Here instead we listen to Advent carols and Advent hymns – from the fourteenth century Irish carol, 'Angelus ad Virginem' telling the story of the angel's visit to the Virgin, to the well known Advent hymn, 'O come, O come Emmanuel'. We hear the evocative sounds of, 'I look from afar and lo, I see the power of God coming' or that beautiful contemporary carol, 'Jesus Christ the Apple Tree'.[3] With such a richness of Advent music we can happily wait until Christmas begins before we sing the familiar carols.

It may surprise some people to know that the cathedrals here and in other places are almost always full for this service. Indeed one English Cathedral, Salisbury, is so famous for its Advent service that people come from all over the world and queue for hours to get a place. There is clearly something powerful about the music and the ritual which resonates with people's own yearnings and speaks to what may be unarticulated needs. This is a ritual which does not need to explain itself: it is what it does. It effects what it signifies. In that sense it is sacramental. Of course there is the aesthetic beauty of the music and the movement. There is the atmospheric space with the darkness illuminated only by candlelight. There is the stillness and the waiting, the sounds of choir and organ and the silences between. There is also, crucially, the communal and shared experience.

What happens here however is not confined to the sacred space of the cathedral; it is not simply a satisfying aesthetic experience but a potentially transformative one. It can reorient people away from that which fails to satisfy and towards a longing for God. It can awaken that spark in the soul as it touches into our darkness and moves us towards the light.

This Advent service and the keeping of Advent time both serve in different ways to mark Advent not simply as 'the run-up to Christmas', but as a preparation for Christ who is to come. The 'once upon a time' is a fairy tale version which sentimental trappings of piety do not displace. 'Christmas is really for the children' we insist as we indulge, and not just in nostalgia. The sweet-faced Madonna with her cherubic baby and nodding animals do not challenge us but are yet another version of the consumer Christmas. Advent awakens in us the 'not yet' which is the other side of the 'already' of the incarnation. It evokes our longing and our hope, 'Let the wilderness and the dry-lands exult, let the wasteland rejoice and blossom.' To terminate this longing on Christmas Day, whether celebrated religiously or commercially, sells us short. Our human experience denies this attempt at closure and insists that the quest continues. Revisiting these themes at the end of this book, I refer to human beings as people who 'cannot get rid of the wish'. We are oriented towards hope. Depression, which is essentially the absence of hope, is seen as a pathological condition. To hope, to look forward, is an essential part of what shapes us as human persons.

For this reason the focus of this short book is not on the liturgical season of Advent itself but on the deep structure of longing, the 'Time of Waiting' which is crystallised in that season, but which is ongoing. Advent is the time of quiet expectancy akin to that quiet just before dawn breaks. It is a time which offers us a 'breathing space'. I have deliberately chosen not to re-

flect on the birth, on Christmas itself, because I want to draw the
longing and the waiting beyond the nostalgic remembrance of
things past to the realisation, in Meister Eckhart's words, that
'The Word is always waiting to be born'.

A colleague described recently how difficult he found it to
'get a handle on Advent'. 'Lent', he explained, 'is a lot easier.
You have a definite penitential theme, and then a clear sequential
narrative during Holy Week. You also have those themes of suffering, death and resurrection, the whole paschal experience
with which people identify.'

Perhaps Advent might be described in terms of space as well
as time. I see it as clearing a space, as 'the work of winter', waiting until the time is right (with apologies to those who live in the
southern hemisphere, who have to translate these images into
their different timeframe!). Is it possible that the male psyche is
more comfortable with a linear model rather than a cyclical one,
with a historical timeline rather than the lunar time of pregnancy,
with death rather than birth as a primary theological resource?
Waiting for birth and waiting for death belong more intimately
together than we usually recognise. Simeon's wisdom has been
lost to us – but so too has the wisdom of Anna and of all women
who have experienced the cycle of life within their own bodies.

I want to turn now to look at the shape of this book in terms
of the stories it tells, the pictures it shows and the poetry on
which it calls.

The Stories: Hearing the Word
As this book arises out of female rather than male experience, it
seemed most appropriate to use the metaphor of pregnancy to
bear this waiting and this hope. I look at this in the opening
chapter. In Chapter 2 instead of turning to the traditional patriarchs and prophets I draw on the female wisdom figures of
Hannah and Elizabeth as Advent's foremothers preparing the
way. In Chapters 3 and 5 I take the familiar texts from Luke of
Annunciation and Visitation and seek not just to retell those
stories but to see how they resonate with contemporary human

experience. I look at the Annunciation story as set within the shelter of Elizabeth's pregnancy. I see it as a story which suggests a sacred space which, to use a phrase of Rowan Williams, 'attunes us to God's communication'.[4] If the Annunciation is about the awakening of the divine spark, the story of the Visitation reveals the fact that we are essentially relational creatures. We all know the effect of words which deaden and drift past us, conversations which never connect, leaving a series of separate sentences, words hanging in the air, rather than an evolving pattern. The spark dies, the conversation is aborted. Then there is the opposite: that lively dialogue, word builds upon word, sentences weave in and out of one another, and so something new emerges. There is also the delight of discovering one who can really listen, who becomes the midwife to that which is struggling to come to birth in us. The Visitation is something like that. It provides the affirmation of what was an internal moment and affirms it. It does more than that – it opens a space where there is hospitality to the new, where the holy can be proclaimed, where grace can be named. You can't do theology alone. You can't be religious alone. Indeed you can't be fully human alone. We depend on one another to call forth what is divine in us as Elizabeth calls it forth in Mary. Chapter 4 bridges the space between Annunciation and Visitation focusing on the journey. This is about leaving the safety of home, setting out, knowing only that nothing will ever be the same again. It looks at the risks of stepping out and the different choices, like those of Ruth and Orpah, to make the journey or to return to the 'mother's house'. The final chapter returns us to the beginning and the idea of waiting for the Word, 'making space for the uncontained God'.

The Pictures: Seeing the Word

In the year 2000 the National Gallery in London mounted an exhibition exploring images of Christ entitled *Seeing Salvation*. I remember going to see it a few weeks after the death of my mother and being very moved by it. For me the gallery was transformed into a sacred space, not simply because of the subject matter, but because of the quality of the attention given to those religious images. It had a unique atmosphere – it was immensely popular and crowds waited patiently to get in but there was a quiet once one was there and, in Britain's secular society, a surprisingly large interest in seeing those masterpieces of Christian art. The purpose was to show the paintings as exploring questions of faith, to see them not so much in terms of art history, in purely formal terms, but in a theological or religious framework. Works from different periods were placed together in conversation as it were, to offer alternative images of similar ideas. Neil MacGregor, then Director of the Gallery, in an introduction to the catalogue accompanying the exhibition, commented on the power of images. He described how the Protestant reformers, suspicious of the image, insisted on the word alone, whereas the Catholic tradition with its rich sacramental understanding had always defended representation. MacGregor offers a contemporary justification: 'Theological concepts must be given human dimension and if only words can tackle abstract mysteries, paintings are uniquely able to address the universal questions through the intelligence of the heart.'[5]

In this felicitous phrase MacGregor recognises that we come to understand not simply through rational thinking but also through a felt intelligence, that of the heart. It is significant that when we have grasped something, the phrase we use to communicate our understanding is 'I see'. Artistic images of theological ideas or scriptural stories should not be seen merely as illustrations, they offer another way of 'seeing'.

Neither should the pictures in this book be viewed as incidental – merely brightening up the text – but as 'illuminations', casting light, offering another way of 'seeing the word'. They serve to take us beyond the word and yet at the same time they take us to where the word is rooted in material reality. There is something of the 'scandalous particularity' of the incarnation in the way in which words become flesh in these paintings. Yet that very particularity gives intensity to the moment which allows it to speak universally. MacGregor talks of how:

In the hands of great artists the different moments and as-
pects of Christ's life become archetypes of all human experience. The Virgin nursing her son conveys the feelings every
mother has for her child: they are love. In the suffering Christ
we encounter the pain of the world and Christ risen and appearing to Mary Magdalene is a universal reaffirmation that
love cannot be destroyed by death.[6]

Thus the work of art becomes a classic, offering fresh insight to
each new generation. This was very clear in the exhibition as
many came unversed in the scriptures and unschooled in the
Christian tradition and yet the paintings spoke to them. The
artist leads us behind the surface to explore the depth dimension
of the experience. Paradoxically we fall back on words again to
try and describe how the painting works. But we do this with a
very firm sense of its inadequacy. Ultimately we might want to
say something like, 'This is what I see. What do you see?' The
power of a work to elicit a response is not limited by a commentary, although sometimes it may be inhibited by it! At its best
such commentary initiates the viewer into the whole process of
attentive looking.

I have become increasingly aware of the power of art to en-
able us to think analogically, symbolically about the mysteries of
faith. Confronted with a painting, of the Annunciation for example, we are much less likely to be caught up in literalism and
more open to the graced imagination at work. The Dominican
artist Kim En Joong refuses even to title his paintings as he wishes
to leave the imagination of the viewer completely free. So in the
case of those paintings, in particular, one can certainly only say,
'This is what I see. What do you see?' I recall being brought before an Aboriginal painting in Australia. 'Don't respond with
your head,' I was told, 'Just let the picture speak to you.' I can
still remember the strong sense of the sacred which the painting
evoked. I recall the 'feeling' when I stayed and simply looked.
MacGregor refers to the fact that the spectators become eye-wit-
nesses to the events. This is very clear in paintings depicting the
passion of Christ where the aim is to evoke pity and compas-

sion. In one painting used in this book, the Fra Angelico Annunciation (plate 2, page 54), we are drawn into the 'sacred space' of the painting. It is once more a present reality. One of the works is contemporary; others are centuries old and yet all are still capable of addressing us now. Their truths are limited neither by the time of their origins nor by the time of the subject matter. They are classic works capable of being perceived differently but equally powerfully, in each generation.

In some ways galleries are like zoos – the paintings are in artificial surroundings, they are in captivity from their place of origin, from the context for which they were created.

In a very real sense the works of art are deracinated: altarpieces removed from churches are now beautifully lit and displayed in surroundings with due attention to humidity and other appropriate conditions for their preservation, yet they look oddly displaced, uprooted from their liturgical space; pieces of frescoes hang on walls looking like limbs amputated from bodies. Paintings intended as singular offerings crowd a wall and jostle for attention. There is of course no touching, so crosses hang in a space cleansed of ambiguity and no lips or hands reach the wounded feet. There is often something almost sterile and ironically artificial in these places.

The exhibition *Seeing Salvation* attempted to redress some of this disconnection by inviting us to see them again in their religious dimension. This did not lessen their power to address the human heart; indeed it may have increased that possibility. This was the purpose for which they were created. Understanding the context alters our perception of them. The paintings chosen here for example reveal very clearly the human dimensions of the experiences described. You can see this in the illustration of the Visitation (plate 3). The scene is so real that you recognise the emotions. It slips its purely spiritual trappings and becomes the human experience of every woman seeking reassurance from another. It is at one and the same time profoundly religious and deeply human. You see. You understand. In paintings such as these the Word becomes flesh and is revealed to us.

The Poetry: Breaking open the Word

In the absence of music, which above all the arts opens us to the transcendent, I have turned instead to poetry which, while continuing to use words, stretches them to their limit and beyond. Poetry, like music, is intended for the ear as well as the eye. Just as the notes on the page call out to be played, to be sung, so the words of the poem call out to be read aloud, to be sounded. The poet too is the one whose very art embodies a 'waiting for the Word'. We look to the poet to 'see things' for us, to take us deeper into the dark and draw us further towards the light. The art of the poet is an evocative one, drawing out from us memories and dreams, hopes and possibilities. Poetry at its best delights and enlightens us. It offers a distilled and imagined transformation of our human experience. The good poem refuses cheap grace and wrestles with the question which may or may not find its resolution. And the poem refuses to be translated into prose. I can even now remember the profound effect of the first poem which evoked that kind of response in me, where to return to MacGregor's phrase, the intelligence of my heart was stirred. This was George Herbert's 'Prayer'.[7] The juxtaposition of different images works to tease the imagination, taking us from one possibility to another: 'the soul in paraphrase, the heart in pilgrimage,' 'reversed thunder, Christ-side-piercing spear' finally coming to rest in 'something understood'. Yet understood in what sense? Not through rational logical progression of argument, but through this evocation of possibility, through the realisation that no single image in itself would suffice but that somehow in the end what prayer is, is understood – and not by us but by the One to whom it is addressed. In this book I turn to contemporary poets sensitive to the pain of the world and yet clear about hope or, in theological terms, about the possibility of redemption, of salvation. Poets such as Denise Levertov are capable of expressing the yearning and the longing, the searching and seeking for Wisdom – that time of waiting for which Advent is the primary metaphor.

CHAPTER ONE

A Time of Waiting

Our time is a time of waiting; waiting is its special destiny. And every time is a time of waiting, waiting for the breaking in of eternity. All time runs forward. All time, both history and in personal life, is expectation. Time itself is waiting, waiting not for another time, but for that which is eternal.[8] Paul Tillich

A radio advertisement I heard recently mocks the idea of waiting. It features a man who apparently enjoys waiting and now his office has bought a new super-fast computer of some sort which means that everything will be done so much faster he won't be able 'to wait'.

Waiting generally has a bad press. We live in a world of immediacy, of 'now'. A selling point is always speed, speed of access, speed of delivery, speed of travel and so on. 'And just tell me' asked the fool, 'what do you intend to do with the extra minutes gained?' And because this was the question of a fool, no one felt the need to respond.

Yet there is a small but growing movement of resistance to this relentless insistence that we must not waste time. In response to the 'fast food' industry there has emerged a 'slow food' movement. There the emphasis is on the quality of the food and the quality of the time spent preparing it and sharing it. I think of one of my favourite films, *Babette's Feast*,[9] telling the story of Babette, a French woman who, when she wins the lottery, decides to prepare a feast for the puritanical Danish community who have given her refuge. She spends weeks in elaborate preparations and all her winnings go towards the splendid meal; she gives them everything she has and the feast becomes a revelation of love. The community is at first shocked by the 'wasteful extravagance' of time and resources but then they realise that this has brought them new life.

Liturgy, as someone once remarked, is simply a waste of time, but then so is prayer, poetry, music, dance and indeed most of life's pleasures! Food and sex are the exceptions in that for humankind they are not merely functional but also potential sources of joy. We do not eat simply in order to live, or have sex solely in order to reproduce ourselves. So we need to ask whether we have matters skewed. Are we made for profit or for pleasure? The order is important. A friend writes to me about a Rabbi she knows. He, not surprisingly, is a man for the Sabbath. He emphasises 'delight' as the essence of Sabbath-keeping! This is far from some rigid notions of what one may not do on 'The Sabbath Day'. Sabbath time is the time of delight in God's grace and freedom summed up by the Rabbi in the possibility of 'eating a whole jar of apricot preserves in one sitting'. In our time we are constricted less by religious mores than by the consumer culture which drives our market and refuses a day of rest. A day of rest is a day without profit. According to a recent publication we are enslaved by consumer desire and our freedom consists of little more than a choice between different products.[10]

If Sabbath time, defined as time to delight in God's glory, to delight in creation, is given priority then other things fall in behind. Time is no longer tyranny but gift. The Sabbath time defines the weekdays just as the feast makes sense of the fast. It all depends where the stress falls. For many the stress never falls away but becomes the norm until the body protests and closes down.

One of my pleasures is making yeast bread. And one of the questions most often asked about it is, 'But doesn't that take a very long time?' Yet a real delight of the process is precisely the time where you wait for the bread to rise. Having mixed the flour and water, the honey and oil, you knead it until you have a smooth ball of dough and as a happy side effect you have also kneaded away your frustrations and stresses. You return from other tasks to risen dough, and punching it down you release the air – along with any residual tension – and shape it into loaves, maybe round, maybe plaited, and leave it to rise yet again. I have given workshops where we have made bread and allowed the rhythm of the process to determine the shape of the day. On these occasions we have discovered something of the reign of God, which is like a woman taking yeast and mixing it with three measures of flour until it is all leavened. It takes time … and we wait … and then we break and we bless and we eat.

I can recall a lecturer once telling us that 'deferred gratification' was a mark of moral maturity. The small child needs everything now. The child cannot wait and one of the major frustrations of its young life is learning to wait. As the child grows she switches her attention to the future but again this is expressed in the language of waiting, 'I can't wait until I'm old enough to … go to school on my own, go to the disco, learn to drive and so on'. 'I can't wait.' Of course too quickly that time does come and by mid-life she is wondering where her youth went.

Paradoxically then, the capacity to wait enables us to live in the present. It suggests that there is no rush, 'we can wait'. The positive images attached to the notion of waiting cluster around images of fidelity and trust. 'I'll be waiting for you,' a mother promises her small child as she leaves her to school. 'I'll wait for you,' a lover promises his beloved as she leaves for an assignment abroad. 'It can wait,' a friend assures another, as they plan to meet. 'Take your time, we'll wait,' a young woman is told as she tries to make up her mind about an important decision. In all of these cases waiting belongs to the language of trust, of promise, of faithfulness. Later on in this book I will look at the idea of 'God waiting'. I will explore this notion with particular reference to a painting by Fra Angelico. I don't want to anticipate the discussion here but suffice to say that what is critical is the sense of human freedom and autonomy which is enabled by the notion of 'God waiting'.

Rowan Williams, the present Archbishop of Canterbury, is

renowned for his pauses before he responds to questions. This is most infuriating for the media, accustomed as they are to the cut and thrust of political debate and the immediate sound bites of the politicians they interview. Silence is not permitted on the airwaves; it is 'dead time', and ironically, used only when someone has died. Rowan Williams is not afraid of silence. He will wait until he has considered the question and then will reply. He talks himself of the importance of listening in 'expectant silence'. He will wait until the other person is ready to speak. A young girl commented recently that a medical consultant waited for her answers when he asked questions. This, in her experience, was unusual – she felt for the first time that someone was listening to her and showing respect for her experience, not rushing in with a ready-made diagnosis.

We fear social silences; few of us will sit in companionable quiet. Few of us will wait and make space for the other to find their true word. Williams uses an example from music therapy with autistic children. The therapist allows the child to make whatever noise she wants to with a series of instruments. Then the therapist gradually becomes aware of a pattern emerging and as it does she echoes what the child is producing. Thus communication begins. 'So it is with our co-operation with the Word of God: we must listen intently for the rhythm of divine life in what may first seem to be unintelligible noise and gradually learn how to echo it and make sounds in union with it.'[11] Something similar happens in music making, perhaps particularly with Jazz. The way in which Jazz musicians can take up and improvise on what the others in the group are playing without having a score implies a deep listening, a felt response, and is a wonderful example not just of technical mastery of music but of a profound level of communication. And when it works it sends shivers down the spine. Watch a string quartet or a chamber choir; they will also demonstrate sensitivity to one another, a listening for what the others are doing which enables them, quite literally, to respond in tune. As one who is relatively unmusical but who happens to live with singers, I am in awe of this

process. Quite often in our own conversations we do the opposite. We wait until the other has finished in order that we may
speak, but with no real sense of having truly heard what has
been said. Couples go to therapists in order to hear, perhaps for
the first time, what their partner is actually saying. The kind of
attention to the other that actually hears 'the word' in them is
unusual. We see this later in the familiar story of the Visitation
and prior to that we look at the 'Waiting for the Word' that is
symbolised in the stories of annunciation to Hannah, to
Elizabeth and then to Mary.

Pregnancy as Slow Time
First though as a significant image of waiting with an expectant
hope, I have chosen the symbol of pregnancy. Pregnancy literally
embodies slow time.

'We have good news,' the young couple say. The listeners
may anticipate but will not spoil their annunciation, 'We're
going to have a baby!'

This very ordinary scene is played out over and over again
and while it is clear that not every pregnancy brings such joy,
many do. Pregnancy, with its mixture of vulnerability, fragility,
but above all expectancy, seems such an appropriate image for
Advent and yet is so rarely called upon. 'She's expecting' is the
shorthand for pregnancy; 'we're expecting' is surely also the
shorthand for Advent.

One of the great ironies about the traditional telling of the
story of the incarnation is how rarely we refer to flesh, to bodies.
A woman came up to me at the end of a reflection on Advent
and said, 'I'm forty-five years old and this is the first time I have
ever heard anyone talk of Mary as pregnant.' Yet Luke's gospel
opens with two pregnant women, two women bearing the hope
of Israel in their bodies. 'The word was made flesh' says John,
but Luke shows the making flesh in female bodies.

The Hebrew scriptures know about births and babies. In fact
Genesis is almost a series of birth announcements, some very
colourful: 'Adah bore Jabal; he was the ancestor of those who

live in tents and have livestock. His brother's name was Jubal; he was the ancestor of all who play the lyre and pipe. Zillah bore Tubal-cain, who made all kinds of bronze and iron tools. The sister of Tubal-cain was Naamah.'[12]

In Genesis we read the familiar story of the conception of Isaac and Sarah's reaction when she heard that they were to have a child when she laughed to herself, saying, 'After I have grown old, and my husband is old, shall I have pleasure?'[13]

So not alone do the scriptures tell of the births of children but they also refer to the pleasure of the sexual act which brings these children into being. As one scholar puts it, 'They know where babies come from.' And yet what is equally clear is the sense that children are a gift, a sign of the covenant, a sign of God's promise for the future, a sign of hope. This is the context in which we understand the births to 'barren' women. Each such birth marks the fact that God is the author of all life – that breath is a gift which is received by the child.

The scripture scholar Walter Brueggemann makes this point, 'All our science has not much advanced beyond the wonder that what is needed for life is indeed given.'[14] He talks about the enduring fragility of human life. We spend much of our time denying this and thus he says we eliminate generosity as a defining feature and requirement of our life.[15] We are formed in God's generosity. Both at the beginning and the end of our lives, we have this sense of fragility, of dependence, and in between there is the illusion of control. But reflection on either our origins or our end should lift that illusion from us.

We begin Lent with the mark of ash on our foreheads: 'Remember, that thou art dust and unto dust shalt thou return.' Perhaps we should begin Advent with a different memory, the memory of having received the breath of life. Dust and breath form us tell the psalmists,

When you take away their breath they die
And return to their dust.
When you send forth your spirit they are created.[16]

We wait for the first cry of the new-born child, the cry that signals this breath and we rejoice, 'I praise you for I am fearfully and wonderfully made.' There are few who visit a new-born child and do not marvel at how 'fearfully and wonderfully' they are made.

The same psalmist has the line, 'For it was you who formed my inward parts; you knit me together in my mother's womb.'[17] Wonder at our origins is deeply connected to hope for the future.

Kathleen Norris has written a poem entitled 'Advent' which begins by describing some pregnant women like Susan, who 'worries that her waters will break / on the subway. New York is full of grandmothers; / someone will take care of her.' She then continues:

Pregnant women stand like sentinels,
they protect me
while I sleep. They part the sea
and pass down the bloody length of it,
until we are strangers
ready to be born,
strangers who will suffer and die.[18]

Although Norris has never been pregnant herself, she praises the 'holy wind' which blows through these women. In this poem she captures both the ordinary wonder of pregnancy and its awkward beauty. Pregnant women are visible, material re-minders of hope for the future so we should not be surprised that they also stand 'like sentinels' at the beginning of the gospel of Luke. They are also physical reminders of the 'enlarging of the tents', of the growing of the womb, of the making space for the child. There is in fact no greater visible image of that need to make space for the new.

As the pregnancy develops the expectant woman has to make many adjustments as to how she dresses, moves, sleeps, eats. It provides an image of generous and hospitable accommod-ation to the 'stranger' growing within. Of course it is not only the pregnant woman who needs to make space for the child, the whole community must make room. The pregnant woman stands as living testimony to the fact that we are created from the beginning in relationship. This is how we are made; this is why we are made. We live in the shelter of one another.

If I seem to place undue stress on this point, I think it is to compensate for how little we have reflected on this primary wonder. I use it now that we might revisit Advent as a time of waiting for birth, not simply for the historical birth of a child at Bethlehem, but the birth of Christ in us. It is we who are called to make space 'for the uncontained God'.

Breathing Time

Pregnancy changes our notion of time. The pregnant woman moves to a different rhythm measured not by what she has achieved or will achieve, but by what is happening within. Days are measured by the changes in the woman's body, by the growth of the child in the womb which modern technology can now show us with startling vividness. Time is measured according to the birth-date which becomes the only fixture which matters. Paradoxically perhaps something similar happens to the menopausal woman but this time it is not the birth of a child which confines her, but the birth of her own soul, which holds her back until the time is right. This is a slower unfolding and there is less exactness about the date and no technology can measure this progress. However this slowing of time, this moving to a different rhythm becomes something that we can practise as Advent time. This of course is deeply ironic as the countdown to Christmas begins earlier and earlier each year, encroaching even on the month of October, colonising the dead days of November until the month of December itself becomes the Christmas rush. Advent pulls against the grain of commerce and offers time as a dimension of depth and stillness rather than a tyranny of the clock or calendar. If we tune into this time we can grow down into the darkness and be there at the point of the turning to the light. Two poets offer their wisdom here. Adrienne Rich talks about waiting and allowing the days to shrink, waiting without sadness, but with a 'grave impatience', she suggests we should 'trust roots'. She calls this the 'work of winter':

The work of winter starts fermenting in my head
how with the hands of a lover or a midwife
to hold back till the time is right

force nothing, be unforced
accept no giant miracles of growth
by counterfeit light[19]

The poet Denise Levertov, in a variation on a theme by Rilke, reflects on the possibility of stillness; she wishes that her senses could take a deep breath and fall silent that her thoughts could be 'filled with you':

and at that timeless moment of possession,
fleeting as a smile, surrender you
and let you flow back into all creation.

And yet she doubts that this can happen and the poem continues:

There will never be that stillness.
Within the pulse of flesh,
in the dust of being where we trudge,
        turning our hungry gaze this way and that,
the wings of the morning
brush through our blood
as cloud-shadows brush the land.
What we desire travels with us.
We must breathe time as fishes breathe water.
God's flight circles us.[20]

Our images of using time, losing time, wasting time, spending time, passing time, making time, all suggest a tyranny of time with the illusion that we are in control and that there is a time-line for our lives, and we must rush headlong towards the goal marked 'end'. Perhaps it doesn't work like that. Students in school see minutes ticking slowly by, students sitting exams see hours flash by. Time speeds up in middle age and slows down again for the elderly. Recently while I was in the supermarket picking up some groceries I met an old man, he was behind me in the queue for the check-out. I had to go back to pick up something I had forgotten and apologised for keeping him waiting. 'But I've all the time in the world', he said, 'Take your time,' and lowering his voice, he confided, 'I was eighty-five last Sunday.'

We notice how time seems to change utterly when we are relaxed and on holiday. It acquires a different dimension and the wise among us put away our watches and don't bring our clocks. Waiting for death alters time, waiting for birth likewise. In all of these cases we live in a different relation to time. We are no longer on time, but in time. Waiting for birth and death we move into cyclical time and recognise the illusory model of the linear progress. We have 'all the time in the world'.

Small children have no sense of time – we say – and the old lose their sense of it – we think. 'What time is it?' my grandmother asked, over and over again as she lay dying. Even then I knew that her question didn't concern the time of the day but the hour of her death for which she waited. As soon as a child is born we record the time, when someone dies we stop the clock. The new-born enters our timeframe, the dying pass beyond it.

Advent returns us to the time of our beginning, and to end-time, to a hope that reaches for the God who was, who is and who is to come:

We must breathe time as fishes breathe water,
God's flight circles us.

CHAPTER TWO

Time to be Surprised by Grace

THE GOOD NEWS ACCORDING TO HANNAH

1 Samuel Chapter 1

There was a certain man of Ramathaim, a Zuphite from the hill country of Ephraim, whose name was Elkanah son of Jeroham, son of Elihu, son of Tohu, son of Zuph, an Ephraimite.

He had two wives; the name of the one was Hannah, and the name of the other Peninnah. Peninnah had children, but Hannah had no children.

Now this man used to go up year by year from his town to worship and to sacrifice to the LORD of hosts at Shiloh, where the two sons of Eli, Hophni and Phineas, were priests of the LORD. On the day when Elkanah sacrificed, he would give portions to his wife Peninnah and to all her sons and daughters; but to Hannah he gave a double portion because he loved her though the LORD had closed her womb. Her rival used to provoke her severely, to irritate her, because the LORD had closed her womb. So it went on year by year; as often as she went up to the house of the LORD, she used to provoke her. Therefore Hannah wept and would not eat. Her husband Elkanah said to her, 'Hannah, why do you weep? And why do you not eat? And why is your heart sad? Am I not more to you than ten sons?'

After they had eaten and drunk in Shiloh, Hannah rose and presented herself before the LORD. Now Eli the priest was sitting on the seat beside the doorpost of the temple of the LORD. She was deeply distressed and prayed to the LORD, and wept bitterly. She made this vow: 'O LORD of hosts, if only you will look on the misery of your servant, and remember me, and not forget your servant, but will give to your servant a male child, then I will set him before

you as a nazirite until the day of his death. He shall drink neither
wine nor intoxicants and no razor shall touch his head.'

As she continued praying before the LORD, Eli observed her
mouth. Hannah was praying silently; only her lips moved, but her
voice was not heard; therefore Eli thought she was drunk. So Eli
said to her, 'How long will you make a drunken spectacle of your-
self? Put away your wine.' But Hannah answered, 'No, my lord, I
am a woman deeply troubled; I have drunk neither wine nor strong
drink, but I have been pouring out my soul before the LORD. Do
not regard your servant as a worthless woman, for I have been
speaking out of my great anxiety and vexation all this time.' Then
Eli answered, 'Go in peace and the God of Israel grant the petition
you have made to him.'

And she said, 'Let your servant find favour in your sight.' Then
the woman went to her quarters, ate and drank with her husband,
and her countenance was sad no longer.

They rose early in the morning and worshiped before the LORD;
then they went back to their house at Ramah. And Elkanah knew
his wife Hannah, and the LORD remembered her.

It seems fitting to begin this Advent journey with the stories
of two ladies-in-waiting. However, the image conjured up by
that phrase – elegant women in a royal household with nothing
better to do than hold a queen's train (or nowadays more likely
her handbag) – just doesn't fit our two women!

Hannah and Elizabeth are two women waiting for birth. One
waits patiently, quietly, reflectively – and prayerfully. The other
waits impatiently, noisily, angrily– and prayerfully. In the case
of Elizabeth, her husband is found dumb and she finds her voice.
In the case of Hannah, Eli the priest is dumbfounded as this
woman teaches him how to pray.

Advent is a time of patient, impatient waiting which reaches
further back than we can remember and further forward than
we can imagine. It gathers our deepest longings for the God who
is, who was and who is to come. Our traditional Advent guides
are Isaiah and John the Baptist but women lurk in the shadows
and in these reflections it is wise women who will guide us,

women like Hannah and Elizabeth, women like Ruth and Naomi, women like Miriam and Mary.

The poet Adrienne Rich begins one of her poems with the line, 'A wild patience has taken me this far.'[21] A similar 'wild patience' has brought Hannah now to a crisis point. She enters the pages of scripture, as most women do, behind her husband, Elkanah, and it is noted, as was customary, that he had two wives, Hannah and Peninnah. One brief sentence tells all: 'Peninnah had children, but Hannah had no children.'[22] We are very quickly drawn into Hannah's distress when we learn that, year by year, her husband went to offer sacrifice and would return with portions for everyone and a double portion for Hannah, 'because he loved her, though the Lord had closed her womb.' However her rival taunts her and Hannah weeps and does not eat. Elkanah is not without pity for her and asks, 'Hannah, why do you weep? Why do you not eat? Am I not more to you than ten sons?'

Like men before him and after him he does not understand this woman and fails to console her.

Hannah's response is to take herself and her weeping from the house to the temple. In fact we are told that 'she presented herself before the Lord' and we note that Eli the priest is sitting on the seat beside the doorpost. If Elkanah is the guardian of the household, Eli is the doorkeeper of the temple. In both cases women depend on the men to grant them their living, to mediate the mysteries, to determine when they come and where they go.

Hannah is deeply distressed and prays and weeps bitterly. For this kind of prayer, no manual will help, no book or scroll contains the words she wants and needs to speak. Hannah knows no rules but the pain and sorrow of her heart and from there she cries out. Pleading for a child she promises that if she is given a son she will consecrate him to the Lord. She uses words that anticipate the prophecy of the angel about John the Baptist, 'He shall drink neither wine nor strong drink and no razor shall touch his head.' Neither husband nor priest can deal with this 'hysterical' woman. Elkanah offered consolation; Eli comes in with words of condemnation. He has been watching her mouth moving but no sound coming out. He thinks she is drunk. 'How long will you make a drunken spectacle of yourself?' he asks. Eli had observed her mouth but he could not read her lips. Later another priest, Zechariah, will be struck dumb by a mystery he cannot fathom; here Eli is deaf to a prayer in a language he does not recognise. Hannah has bypassed the priest, the mediator of the mysteries, and spoken directly to God, with a prayer that comes straight from the gut, the same source as God's compassion. Hannah is not quoting the prophets, or reading from Eli's scrolls. She is praying from the depths of her soul, a prayer that has gone too deep for words. Perhaps what Eli witnessed, and was shocked by, was the silent scream of anguish.

Men cannot deal with 'hysterical' women and these cries come from the *hystera*, the womb. For Hannah has opened her mouth to pray that the mouth of her womb should be opened.

But when Hannah turns from her prayer to respond to Eli, he is as discomfited by her reply as he was shocked by her prayer, for she gives a perfectly logical and rational interpretation of her state. Quite matter-of-factly she puts him right: 'No, my lord, I am a woman deeply troubled; I have drunk neither wine nor strong drink, but I have been pouring out my soul before the Lord. Do not regard your servant as a worthless woman, for I have been speaking out of my great anxiety and vexation all this time.' It is interesting that she does not reveal the subject of her prayer, which remains a matter between herself and the 'Lord of hosts'. Eli, completely wrong footed, stutters his reply attempting to contain Hannah's passionate prayer in a formulaic response and bring the petition back under his control: 'Go in peace; the God of Israel grant the petition you have made to him.' Her reply, 'Let your servant find favour in your sight,' completes the restoration of order and decorum. Hannah shrinks back to the traditional role of humble petitioner and Eli resumes his role as keeper of the holy places.

Yet this has been a transformative moment for Hannah. We are told that she returned home and ate and drank with her husband, and 'her countenance was sad no longer'. The depression she had experienced has been eased by the expression of her pain. The following morning Hannah and Elkanah worship together and 'Then they went back to their house at Ramah. Elkanah knew his wife Hannah, and the Lord remembered her.' Putting a gloss on that we see a couple who having eaten and drunk together cheerfully, and slept well, then go and pray together before returning home and making passionate love, no doubt as passionate as the prayer of the previous day. This is not a fumbling in the dark, a reaching out merely to satisfy the needs of the flesh, a coupling that scarcely merits the term love-making, but a true knowing of one-another. Is it any wonder that a child is conceived! Human desire meets divine response. Relationships have been restored.

There is no hint of dualism here between flesh and spirit. Instead we have a wonderful rhythm where the prayer to conceive is followed by the act of making love. The conversation with the Lord is followed by conversation between the lovers. The prayer becomes performative. Hannah teaches us how to pray.

The child is named Samuel with the simple explanation, 'I asked him of the Lord.'

Hannah, having asked the Lord for a child, keeps her promise and returns him to the Lord, reminding Eli – as if he could forget – 'I am the woman who was standing here in your presence, praying to the Lord. For this child I prayed and the Lord granted me the petition I made to him. Therefore I have lent him to the Lord; as long as he lives, he is given to the Lord.'

Hannah, from being an oppressed woman, barren and without standing or status, has become a woman who, having received the gift of the birth of a child has the freedom to return that gift. To our contemporary eyes this may seem odd but to her it is perfectly rational: she does not possess this child, she does not own him; he is temporarily given into her care. It is thus with all our children but we have greater difficulty in recognising it, and often view our children as extensions of ourselves rather than as persons in their own right. Hannah proves herself able to pray not only out of pain and lament – and probably anger, but also to praise. She sings her song of exultation, a song-line which will echo down the centuries and be taken up later by Miriam of Nazareth, 'My heart exults in the Lord; my strength exults in my God.'

Hannah announces to the people that the Lord is on the side of the oppressed, 'The bows of the mighty are broken, but the feeble gird on strength. Those who were full have hired themselves out for bread; those who were hungry are fat with spoil. He raises up the poor from the dust; he lifts the needy from the ash heap.' Hannah knows these things; she has experienced them in her own body, this is a word made flesh in her.

Hannah is Advent's foremother, Advent's grandmother. It is her wisdom we hearken to when things seem impossible. She is the foremother of Advent waiting, of Advent hope, of prayer without ceasing, of embodied passionate prayer. In her the whole body shapes itself into a longing. She teaches us to trust. She teaches us that there are times – and this may be one of them – when we have to forge a new language. There are times – and this may be such a time – when the words of priests and politicians seem threadbare as they repeat worn-out mantras and mouth clichés. There are times – and this may be such a time – to lay aside the scrolls and missals, the manifestos and mission statements, and discover and uncover with Hannah the language of our deepest desires, the language of our soul. Our barrenness may be of the soul rather than of the flesh but it is nonetheless painful as we long to be nourished and to bring something new to birth.

Hannah is truly the prophet of Advent hope. She is caught between the place her husband has given her and the place the priest has ordained for her, the place the culture has designated for her and the language of limitation she has learnt. And yet she seeks out her own place and shapes it to fit that hope.

She does not dare at first to speak aloud. We see the silent scream which so distresses Eli. It fits no manual on prayer which he has studied. She trusts in a God beyond limitation and she trusts even without the promise of her prayer being granted. No angel comes to Hannah, or indeed to Elkanah. But as confident as a woman who tells her husband that now would be a good time to make love, Hannah trusts. The voice blocked by pain is finally released in song, 'My heart exults in the Lord.'

THE GOOD NEWS ACCORDING TO ELIZABETH

Luke Chapter 1

In the days of King Herod of Judea, there was a priest named Zechariah, who belonged to the priestly order of Abijah. His wife was a descendant of Aaron, and her name was Elizabeth. Both of them were righteous before God, living blamelessly according to all the commandments and regulations of the Lord. But they had no children because Elizabeth was barren, and both were getting on in years.

Once when he was serving as priest before God and his section was on duty, he was chosen by lot according to the custom of the priesthood, to enter the sanctuary of the Lord and offer incense. Now at the time of the incense offering, the whole assembly of the people was praying outside. Then there appeared to him an angel of the Lord standing on the right side of the altar of incense. When Zechariah saw him he was terrified and fear overwhelmed him. But the angel said to him, 'Do not be afraid, Zechariah, for your prayer has been heard. Your wife Elizabeth will bear you a son, and you will name him John. You will have joy and gladness, and many will rejoice at his birth, for he will be great in the sight of the Lord. He must never drink wine or strong drink; even before his birth he will be filled with the Holy Spirit. He will turn many of the people of Israel to the Lord their God. With the spirit and power of Elijah he will go before him, to turn the hearts of parents to their children, and the disobedient to the wisdom of the righteous, to make ready a people prepared for the Lord.' Zechariah said to the angel, 'How will I know that this is so? For I am an old man, and my wife is getting on in years.' The angel replied, 'I am Gabriel. I stand in the presence of God, and I have been sent to speak to you, and to bring you this good news. But now, because you did not believe my words which will be fulfilled in their time, you will become mute, unable to speak, until the day these things occur.'

Meanwhile the people were waiting for Zechariah, and wondered at his delay in the temple. When he did come out, he could not speak to them, and they realised that he had seen a vision in the sanctuary. He kept motioning to them and remained unable to speak. When his time of service was ended, he went to his home.

After those days his wife Elizabeth conceived, and for five months she remained in seclusion. She said, 'This is what the Lord has done for me in the days when he looked favourably on me, and took away the disgrace I have endured among my people.'

Elisheba was the wife of Aaron[23] and Elizabeth is a descendant of Aaron and so she enters scripture bearing an important lineage. Matters begin quietly, even auspiciously: we are told that 'both of them were righteous before God, living blamelessly according to all the commandments.'[24] Then comes the 'But'– 'But they had no children, because Elizabeth was barren and both were getting on in years.' Even here there remains some vestige of the original equality – both were old – but yet the blame for their childless state is attributed primarily to Elizabeth.

In contrast to Hannah, Elizabeth is quiet. Perhaps her days of weeping are over and she has learnt acceptance, even resignation. Perhaps with no rival to taunt her she can pass over the monthly reminder of her childless state and now waits for the ceasing of her periods which will no longer signal birth, but menopause.

So in this story it is not Elizabeth who goes to the temple to pour out her soul, but Zechariah who goes because it is his turn to offer incense. Is Elizabeth among the crowd praying outside, or has she remained at home? We don't know.

Zechariah is simply carrying out the duty assigned to him by lot when the angel appears. His reaction is typical and appropriate: terror and fear overwhelm him.

The angel promises a child, telling him that his prayers have been answered, that he will have joy and gladness, that the child will be full of the Holy Spirit and so on. Zechariah feels old, not just too old for child bearing and rearing, but for miracles, and protests as much: 'I am an old man; my wife is getting on in years.'

For failing to hear 'the good news' and seeing only the obstacles, for too much doubt and too little wonder, Zechariah is struck dumb.

The picture of the priest, the man of words, emerging from the temple and experiencing the pain and humiliation of muteness is a graphic one.

But the effect of this is to create a space – the space opened up by the absence of speech enables Zechariah to draw closer to the God he had perhaps contained too easily in prayers, readings and ritual. Perhaps he was so busy addressing God there was no room for God to speak to him. So he is given a space for contemplation, an Advent space of waiting to find God in stillness, in silence, in the house and not in the temple. And so he returns home.

The drama in that tale is such that everyone hearing it remembers the effect of the annunciation of the birth of John the Baptist: Zechariah is struck dumb. But if we ask 'What happened to Elizabeth?' It is not simply Zechariah who is dumb. There is silence and we all become mute: 'What does happen to her?'

Accustomed as we are to focusing on the male heroes of the story we slip over the response of Elizabeth. We fail to notice that while Zechariah loses his power of speech, Elizabeth finds her voice. In fact after Zechariah is silenced the narrative turns to her: 'After those days his wife Elizabeth conceived, and for five months remained in seclusion. She said, "This is what the Lord has done for me when he looked favourably upon me and took away the disgrace I have endured among my people".' There is a marked contrast between the response of Elizabeth and that of Zechariah, and feminist commentators note how quickly and easily Elizabeth 'recognises God's grace'.[25] I think there are several reasons for this. For the first time we get a sense of how Elizabeth has suffered when she refers to 'the disgrace' she has endured among the people. Revealed in these lines is the pain that was hidden behind the earlier comment, 'Elizabeth was barren.' Yet at the same time she had been described by the narrator as 'righteous' and 'blameless', so in some ways there is some ambivalence here. Which reading of her life had she accepted? Had she continued to trust in God despite the blame and shame of the people around her? Is it that trust which now enables her to understand what has happened to her as 'good news'? And so as 'disgrace' is removed, Elizabeth names what has happened to her as 'grace': the 'good news' announced by the angel to Zechariah is proclaimed first by Elizabeth. This is no cheap grace, it has come out of sorrow and lament, it has come out of years of suffering; this is a hard won grace and now it comes after five months of prayerful meditation before she speaks. Her awareness of the life growing within her sharpens the intensity with which she can hear the living voice of God. And thus she interprets her experience as grace-filled. I wonder too whether Zechariah's muteness is not a way of bringing him through some of the pain and humiliation his wife had suffered, in order that he might be purged of his doubts and be ready, with a pure heart, to receive 'the good news'.

There is no explicit account in this text as there was in the story of Hannah, of any love-making which would result in the pregnancy. There is none of the poignancy of that story – of a relationship restored. Yet we may assume that this miracle does not bypass human action. Perhaps we can fill in the gaps. We may imagine that having been deprived of the language of speech, they turn to the language of touch, and so the blessing and promise are communicated, as intended, through their bodies, and once again the word is made flesh.

Elizabeth at first withdraws into her own space to reflect on what has happened. Pregnancy turns a woman inwards as she wonders at the changes in her body and the new life growing within. It is the most extraordinary ordinary miracle. In many ways the biblical accounts of barren women conceiving serve in the first instance to highlight the miracle of every pregnancy. The period of five months also allows the pregnancy to move out of the vulnerable and fragile early weeks when miscarriages more easily occur. Elizabeth may have suffered early miscarriages in previous pregnancies, all failures gathered under the shameful banner of 'barren'. By the time she is ready to announce it, her body has changed, and the pregnancy is visible and so she can say, 'Look what the Lord has done for me!' And she walks proudly among her people. Her confinement becomes her liberation.

As any pregnant woman knows, time changes and is no longer measured by external events but by what is occurring within. The deadlines of jobs to be completed become the lifelines of the changes each week brings. And so in the gospel of Luke the lines drawn to frame the story historically, 'In the days of King Herod of Judea', are momentarily set aside and replaced by a lunar timescale, by the time of gestation, by time for birth. Instead of forty days in the wilderness, we have forty weeks of fruitfulness.

And so almost imperceptibly we become aware that Elizabeth's pregnancy shapes the story of the annunciation to Mary. Those familiar first lines, 'In the sixth month' could have the phrase 'of Elizabeth's pregnancy' added to them. This has the effect of taking that so familiar and almost ethereal story of an angelic visitation and grounding it in the very human story of another woman's pregnancy. More importantly perhaps it places Mary in the shelter of the older woman. But before we move on to discuss that second annunciation, let us return to Elizabeth and consider her role as an Advent foremother.

As one who bears the contradictions of 'righteous', 'blameless' yet barren, Elizabeth has had to learn the art of detachment from expectation. She has had to ground herself in her faith and in a trusting relationship with God. Happiness, says the contemporary guru, is all about status. Wife of a priest confers status, barrenness takes it away. Elizabeth has had to learn to live with the contradictions and find a still centre within.

She shows none of the feisty energy of Hannah, nothing of

her passionate outpouring, of her impatient waiting, but just as much as Hannah, she understands prayer and praise. Most of all she recognises God, not as one who desires her suffering, but rather as one who wishes for her joy. She does not hold God responsible for her suffering, but for her salvation. He has taken away 'the disgrace I have endured among my people.'

Elizabeth and Zechariah in their time of silent retreat come to reflect on a God who is not controlled or confined, but who is essentially a 'God of surprises'. Elizabeth has never lost her trust in this God, to whom she remained faithful, despite all vicissitudes.

Zechariah, on the other hand, had clearly continued to pray that they might be blessed with a child. 'Your prayer has been heard' the angel says, but his prayer had become a matter of rote in which he himself no longer believed: 'I am an old man.' Be careful for what you pray, it might just be granted! Zechariah, like many of us, is more comfortable with the burden, to which he has become accustomed, than with its removal, which will bring new responsibilities.

Elizabeth believes that with God, all things are possible. Zechariah learns it. And when his tongue is loosened again he too pours forth a song of praise.

The pattern of barren wives is a common motif, a powerful image for the God of reversals; the God of surprising grace. It serves as a reminder of the graced event of every pregnancy, reminding us that, despite the language of choice and rights, every child is gift and grace embodied. Sarah laughed when she heard she was pregnant, Hannah wept when she knew she was not; there is much emotion attached to this state. Elizabeth is more measured in her response but later when she encounters her pregnant cousin her joy is given full release and voice.

Elizabeth is the first to prepare the way: she prepares the way for Zechariah who learns through her; later she prepares the way for Mary, as John the Baptist prepares the way for Jesus. John the Baptist will spend time in the desert, but Elizabeth has been in the wilderness for years. He will call the people to repentance, but she is the first to announce the 'good news to the poor'.

As an Advent foremother she teaches us trust, attentive listening, careful watching so that we do not miss the blessings around us. She teaches us not to depend on the judgements of others but to find that centre of the self which is secure in the knowledge of having been loved into existence by a gracious God. Finally, having been surprised by grace, she is the one who can name grace for others.

Both Hannah and Elizabeth teach us something about prayer. The Dominican Herbert McCabe says that prayer is the first way we show we have hope, trust in God and trust in the future, and that is what Advent is essentially about.[26] A child pre-eminently symbolises hope for the future, so to pray for a child, to pray for birth is a material, bodily expression of that hope. People talk about hope having wings, but here hope takes flesh. What makes Hannah's prayer so profound is that she lays bare her genuine desires. McCabe talks about the fact that many people complain of distraction in prayer, but he says that this is because people tend to pray for things they think they ought to want, ignoring their true desires which then surface. He notes that people on sinking ships don't tend to complain of distractions.[27] It is this absolute concentration in Hannah which so unsettles the priest, Eli.

In the case of Zechariah, we see someone who has lost touch with his desire and his prayer has become formulaic. His punishment of muteness gives him the chance to listen again, to get in touch again with the desires of his heart, and so to learn to pray. Learning to pray makes him ready to receive the gift he so nearly rejected.

Elizabeth exhibits a real understanding of the gift, as in turn does Mary, by her receptivity. Grace, by its nature, is unexpected, is surprise. It cannot come to those who exercise such control over themselves and over others that they leave no room for the odd and surprising work of grace. They do not allow themselves to be caught unawares.

Maybe Advent is a time to make space to be caught unawares.

The Meeting at the Golden Gate by Giotto Di Bondone (1266/7-1337) (plate 1, page 49)

In the Arena Chapel in Padua, the artist Giotto has painted wonderful frescoes of the life of the Virgin, including many scenes from the apocryphal gospels. One fresco depicts the meeting of Joachim and Anna, traditionally the parents of Mary, at the Golden Gate. Joachim had withdrawn to the wilderness for forty days because his offering at the temple had been rejected because he was childless. Then an angel appeared to Anna and told her that she would conceive. Joachim had a similar vision and so he returns home with joy. Their encounter at the Golden Gate is an immensely tender scene as Anna's hand caresses the bearded face, and his arm enfolds her in an embrace. It is a beautiful image of conjugal love between two people 'getting on in years'! This is the image I am transposing to the similar story of Zechariah and Elizabeth. Indeed it also speaks to the story of Hannah and Elkanah. This embrace between Joachim and Anna has a universal significance which transcends the particularity of its image. It suggests the restoration of a relationship, the healing of the pain of separation.

Giotto di Bondone is accepted as being the starting point for art that is naturalistic, full of dramatic narrative and imbued with psychological insight.[28] All of these qualities are to be seen in the Arena Chapel in Padua which tells the story in frescoes of the life of Christ, prefaced by the life of the Virgin. The frescoes are arranged in three tiers. The top tier tells the story of Joachim and Anna and the Nativity and life of Mary, the second tier goes from the birth of Jesus to his ministry and miracles, and the bottom tier tells the story from the passion to the resurrection. Each scene is a complete drama and some are very moving.

The frescoes telling of Joachim and Anna are based on stories in the apocryphal gospels, possibly derived originally from the story of the birth of Samuel to Hannah. In contrast to the story of Hannah, the artist focuses on the sorrow and humiliation of the male character rather than the female. The first time we see

Anna, she is at prayer – exhibiting a quiet resignation, like that of Elizabeth perhaps?

The meeting with her husband reveals her emotion. As with Elizabeth disgrace is displaced by grace. Here too grace is embodied in the physical encounter. What we see in the illustration is the detail of the embrace. This is set in a scene with a shepherd boy to the left, and a group of women to the right, including a mysterious veiled lady dressed in black appearing almost as a harbinger of death, even as birth is announced.

They stand just to the left of a golden arch. The curved arch, apart from suggesting Giotto's familiarity with classical monuments, may also symbolise the womb.

However, it is the actual embrace that I want to look at. Slightly left of centre, and yet the focal point of the scene, we can't take our eyes away from the couple. This is a full embrace: their lips touch, Anna's right hand reaches round the back of Joachim's head and her left hand tenderly strokes his bearded face. His arms reach out to enfold her. His face half covers hers, as the two become one; we see two eyes: one his, one hers, we see one nose, his, one pair of lips, hers. Her already full clothing anticipates the fullness of pregnancy. In the wilderness his cloak had fallen loosely about him, as if mimicking his despair, while here it is gathered up again in elegant folds and his arm is freed to embrace his wife. We notice too the mutuality in the embrace: there is no dominance of male over female; their heads are almost the same height. The group surrounding the couple, the women following Anna, the shepherd boy with Joachim, all gather around as if to witness a marriage, or in this case to see the renewal of marriage vows, which this becomes. It is interesting that the embrace focuses on the faces of each of this elderly pair. The first thing an infant recognises is the face of its mother or father, the child smiles, from that moment on the child searches for faces. The first crude drawing a small child makes is often of a house which resembles a face with its windows and door. A child sitting on her parent's lap will seek to turn the mother's face towards her. My daughter remembers how her grandmother's greeting was to hold the child's face in her large warm hands. Friends who are separated long to meet again, face to face. The Hebrew scriptures talk about the possibility and impossibility of seeing the face of God. The psalmists speak about 'seeking the face of God' and Psalm 67 tells of God's graciousness and blessing, asking that God's face may shine upon us. The plea of the sinner is that God's face will be not be hidden.[29] We talk about facing death, facing the future and so on. Here the two elderly lovers meet after their long absence, and Anna reaches out to hold the face of her beloved Joachim. This is an image which is at the same time utterly human and deeply spiritual. The artist conveys the depth of love and compassion which heals the relationship.

It is interesting that the faces do not convey great joy. In fact the smiles are on the faces of the watching women, but they convey something deeper, a love which has suffered and endured.

Like all great art, this image transcends the particularity of its context. Joachim's meeting with Anna at the Golden Gate becomes a metaphor for conjugal love; it also becomes an image of a relationship restored. In the gospels, and depicted by many artists, we have the image of the father embracing the prodigal son, a relationship restored after the rupture of sin. Artists also depict the embrace of Mary and Elizabeth, as we shall see. This is a rare example of the embrace between a husband and wife.

It fits the stories we have been discussing: firstly restoration of the relationship between Hannah and Elkanah. In that case she had been the one in the wilderness, metaphorically at least, and now she returns to a full relationship and to a love-making which will result in the conception of a child. Secondly we can imagine the meeting between Zechariah and Elizabeth in a similar way: he is the one humiliated, she is the one who knows what it is to be 'disgraced'. They meet and embrace and she reaches out to him in understanding and love. Deprived of the language of speech, they use the language of touch, and thus, the promise of the angel is consummated.

Finally it seems to me that in a culture such as ours where the dominant imagery is about sex disconnected from love, where the dominant culture is that of youth, where the notion that two people 'getting on in years' might feel passionately about one another would be laughable, if not actually taboo, then this image restores that possibility and testifies to an enduring love. It bears witness to a love that survives separation and sorrow, pain and humiliation; it bears witness to a love that is patient and kind; it bears witness to a love which does not deny, but celebrates sexuality. In the Hebrew scriptures the image of conjugal love occurs as a metaphor both to depict the falling away from God and the return to God. Quite often this is used in a sexist manner, with the woman invariably being the one to fall away, as in the book of Hosea for example. However in these stories, and in this painting, the essential complementarity between the pairs offers another image of God, male and female, through the rhetoric of sexuality.[30] The love celebrated most explicitly in the story of Hannah and Elkanah, and visually depicted in the painting of Joachim and Anna and presupposed between Zechariah and Elizabeth, is 'bone of bone and flesh of flesh.'[31] In each case a child is conceived but the love relationship is prior to that – and transcends it: 'Am I not more to you than seven sons?' Elkanah had asked of Hannah. Ultimately it images the love of God.

We've spoken about sacred spaces. Each of the characters has experienced a space apart, a space to listen to the voice of God speaking to them in their distress: in their anguish as with Hannah, Anna and Joachim, in their weariness as with Zechariah, or in their patient endurance as with Elizabeth. That time was followed by a coming together in a transformed relationship. Here this is depicted by the meeting at the gate of the temple. We tend to think of the temple as the 'sacred space' but the ground on which this couple meet and embrace becomes itself a sacred space of love transformed, love renewed, love turned with hope towards the future. In a similar way it is outside the temple in the domestic space that Zechariah too learns again to trust. Words are here made flesh. Almost like the steps of a dance we shall see a similar movement of withdrawal and advance, separation and connection, when we turn now to look at the scenes of the Annunciation and Visitation.

CHAPTER THREE

And the Angel Waited: Breathing Time

Luke Chapter 1

> *In the sixth month the angel Gabriel was sent from God to a town in Galilee called Nazareth, to a virgin engaged to a man whose name was Joseph, of the house of David. The virgin's name was Mary. And he came to her and said, 'Greetings, favoured one. The Lord is with you!'*
>
> *But she was much perplexed by his words, and pondered what sort of greeting this might be.*
>
> *The angel said to her, 'Do not be afraid, Mary, for you have found favour with God. And now, you will conceive in your womb and bear a son, and you will name him Jesus. He will be great, and will be called the Son of the Most High; and the Lord God will give to him the throne of his ancestor David. He will reign over the house of Jacob for ever; and of his kingdom there will be no end.' Mary said to the angel, 'How can this be, since I am a virgin?' The angel said to her, 'The Holy Spirit will come upon you, and the power of the Most High will overshadow you; therefore the child to be born will be holy; he will be called Son of God. And now, your relative Elizabeth in her old age has also conceived a son; and this is the sixth month for her who was said to be barren. For nothing will be impossible with God.' Then Mary said, 'Here am I the servant of the Lord; let it be with me according to your word.' Then the angel departed from her.*

There is nothing of the humorous folk-tale of the Hannah story or the poignancy of Elizabeth's story in this text, but there is the skill of the artist Luke weaving this episode of divine visitation into Elizabeth's story so that she becomes its human shelter. The great Dominican mystic Meister Eckhart begins his sermon on the Annunciation in the following way:

St Luke writes these words: 'At that time the angel Gabriel was sent by God.' At what time? 'In the sixth month,' when John the Baptist was in his mother's womb.

If someone were to ask me why do we pray, why do we fast, why do we all perform our devotions and good works, why are we baptised, why did God, the All-Highest, take on our flesh? Then I would reply: in order that God may be born in the soul, and the soul born in God. That is why the whole of scripture was written and why God created the whole world, and all the orders of angels, that God could be born in the soul and the soul in God.[32]

Something interesting is going on here. On the one hand Eckhart situates the moment of Annunciation quite precisely – 'In the sixth month when John the Baptist was in his mother's womb' – and that in itself is significant, that time is given the dimensions of the womb; on the other hand Eckhart swiftly moves from the particular event of the Angel Gabriel and Mary to talk about God's birth in the soul. Eckhart seems to ask, 'What use is it to talk about Mary giving birth to Christ unless we do likewise?'

I want to follow Eckhart's line and read this story symbolically. Artists and poets have opened up the possibilities of the Annunciation story and enabled me to reappropriate it after years of resistance to its attendant pieties. Now I scour the galleries of every new city I visit, lighting on different versions of this so often painted theme. There is almost always a concentration on the central moment of the encounter between the angel and Mary. Yet around the edges of the story – framing it as it were – is Elizabeth's pregnancy. In my, albeit limited, experience this is never shown. The angel and the virgin stand alone. This is often depicted as a mystical experience but the poet Charles Causley in his 'Ballad of the Breadman' is more direct and domestic:

Mary stood in the kitchen
    Baking a loaf of bread.
An angel flew in through the window.
    'We've a job for you,' he said.[33]

The poet Denise Levertov describes the more traditional set-ting in her poem 'Annunciation' which opens:

We know the scene: the room variously furnished,
almost always a lectern, a book; always
the tall lily.

Arrived on solemn grandeur of great wings,
the angelic ambassador, standing or hovering,
whom she acknowledges, a guest.

Both poets in radically different ways are aware of the paral-ysis of the imagination in relation to this most familiar story. It is difficult to get behind the patina of piety; it is equally difficult to reach it from beneath the weight of interpretation which bears down on these few verses. There is no innocent route. This is perhaps why we turn to artists who, although also part of their culture, by virtue of their gift, inevitably transcend it.

But the first artist is Luke himself and perhaps acknowledg-ing that would help us. His poetry – and what other mode could one use to describe the encounter between the Spirit of God and this woman? – is gracefully imagined. Luke takes an internal moment of 'call and response' and shapes it, and gives it flesh. Exegetes have taken each word and traced it back to its usage and origin in the Hebrew scriptures, literalists have taken each word and nailed down its meaning, theologians have taken each word and interpreted its sense and provided doctrines, and in all this we have learnt much and unlearnt more. Only poets, artists and musicians have felt at liberty to play. Yet what is im-plied in this text is a moment of utter creativity. Theologian and Anglican priest, John Drury says of Luke's imaginative powers in this text, 'It can only be imaginary, but it is controlled by a firm and delicate sense of the incongruity of its two participants, held together over a respectful distance by their mutual regard … So the words hover around an event: promising it, question-ing it and explaining it in a courteous confluence of the practical and the miraculous, the domestic and the strange.'[35]

In this conversation I look for partners who will appreciate the delicacy of the exchange. I find this particularly in the poet

Denise Levertov and in the translucent beauty of the paintings
of Fra Angelico. Both work with the 'intelligence of the heart'.

When I first think of this text, I hear a child's voice, probably
my own, reciting the passage, 'In the sixth month the angel
Gabriel was sent by God ...' We had to learn it by heart and so it
entered the bloodstream. There was without doubt, a rediscov-
ery for me in relation to a text which had lain buried for so long
in the depths of my sub-conscious, occasionally taken out and
interrogated under various guises, the most recent being the
guise or guide of feminist theology. However, it was not until the
encounters with works of art that a true re-cognition occurred
and I knew the story again 'by heart'.

Levertov introduces her poem with a compelling line from
the Agathistos hymn, 'Hail, space for the uncontained God.' I
was so taken with this image and all that it suggested that I felt it
could provide the metaphor to carry the Advent theme which
seemed to me to be about making space for the birth of Christ. I
also found it to be a wonderfully rich title for Mary, who pre-
eminently, generously, becomes that space. Other titles suggest
a similar idea – Ark of the Covenant and so on – but not so
provocatively.

The moment on which Levertov focuses in her poem is that
moment of waiting. She insists on Mary's freedom and her
courage which 'no one mentions'.

'God waited' she says and leaves the line hanging, suspended
while she glosses:

> She was free
> to accept or to refuse, choice
> integral to humanness.

―――――――――――

She draws a line as if to emphasise the pause. As we shall see
when we look at works of art, almost without exception every
artist portrays the scene of the Annunciation with a space which
is carefully delineated between the angel and Mary. A strong
visual sense of waiting is portrayed along with a very marked

Plate 1: *The Meeting at the Golden Gate,* c.1305 (fresco) *Gate in Jerusalem,*
c.1305 (fresco) by Giotto di Bondone (c.1266-1337)
Scrovegni (Arena) Chapel, Padua, Italy / www.bridgeman.co.uk

sense of a sacred space which will not be transgressed. Elizabeth
Johnson in her recent book on Mary suggests that the scene follows the literary structure both of a birth announcement story
and of a prophetic commissioning, with one exception – Mary's
direct response. Ironically then she points out that the very response suggesting human freedom and autonomy has been
used ever since to place women in stances of passivity, submis-
siveness, and self-negation: 'Behold the handmaid of the Lord,
be it done unto me according to Thy word.' Women theologians
now question this interpretation and talk back to the culture of
Luke which accepted the master-slave relationship suggested in:
'Here am I the servant or slave of the Lord.' Reading against the
grain of the text they subvert it and find a liberating message in

Mary's courage, in her empowerment, illustrated later through
the *Magnificat*. But first we go back to the poet. Denise Levertov
paints the scene onto a broader canvas, asking whether there are
not annunciations of one sort or another in most lives?

> Some unwillingly
> undertake great destinies,
> enact them in sullen pride,
> uncomprehending.
> More often
> those moments
>   when roads of light and storm
>   open from darkness in a man or woman,
> are turned away from
> in dread, in a wave of weakness, in despair
> and with relief.
> Ordinary lives continue.
> God does not smite them.
> But the gates close, the pathway vanishes.

———————————

Once more that line is drawn but here it indicates the closing
off of possibility. The poet then considers the destiny to which
this woman was called:

> to bear in her womb
> Infinite weight and lightness; to carry
> in hidden, finite inwardness,
> nine months of Eternity ...

What interests Levertov though is the moment of which no
one speaks, the moment when she could still refuse. Once more
the shaping of the poem reflects the pause, the suspension,

> A breath unbreathed,
> Spirit,
> suspended,
> waiting.

———————————

For the last time the line is drawn under these words as if to insist on that long moment, that sacred space, when Gabriel waits and the virgin 'ponders these things in her heart'. Perhaps this is the moment frozen in time in Fra Angelico's painting?

The child I was, reciting the text by heart, and knowing it was near the end, gabbled on from 'For nothing is impossible with God' to 'Then Mary said'. The woman I now am allows that pause, and I too hold my breath and wait for the assent: 'Let it be with me.' For this is a space, pregnant with possibility. This is the grace note of silence, the moment of deepest contemplation; this above all is the Advent moment. And so the poem may end:

She did not cry, 'I cannot, I am not worthy,'
nor, 'I have not the strength.'
She did not submit with gritted teeth,

       raging, coerced.
Bravest of all humans,

     consent illumined her.
The room filled with its light,
the lily glowed in it,

    and the iridescent wings.
Consent,

   courage unparalleled,
opened her utterly.

Shifting the emphasis to the moment of human response rather than divine initiative restores the balance and allows us to see this woman not as a passive vessel – which is how women were viewed – but as the essential partner in this drama.

This is of course precisely where the text speaks most deeply to us. Divine call depends on human response. Zechariah stutters and then loses his voice, but Mary – like Elizabeth – finds hers. If we experienced prayer as powerful pleading and crying out in the Hannah story, here we have prayer as profound listening, moving through the typical modes of fear and questioning, assurance and finally acceptance. It is interesting too that the assurance provided brings us back to the sheltering presence of Elizabeth who hovers behind the scenes, almost like Sarah, hiding to hear what message the visitors were bringing to

Abraham. Elizabeth is of course not actually present, but her pregnancy provides both the timescale and the ultimate assurance: 'And now your relative Elizabeth in her old age has also conceived a son; and this is the sixth month for her who was said to be barren.' The promise to Mary is that she will be empowered and protected by God, and the annunciation of one birth is sealed by the evidence of another. As contemporary theologians confirm, there are no sexual connotations in this scene, we simply do not know what happened. However, we can recognise the religious import of the encounter. Elizabeth Johnson describes it as '… a theophany. It places this woman in deep attentive relation to the Spirit of God.'[36]

Others speculate about illegitimacy but that scandal is implied more in the account of Matthew than Luke. Charles Causley suggests it in his ballad,

> Joseph was in the workshop
>> Planing a piece of wood.
> 'The old man's past it,' the neighbours said.
>> 'That girl's been up to no good.'

It is clear that Luke wants to make a dramatic statement which will supersede the event of the previous story. As John the Baptist prepares the way for Jesus, Elizabeth prepares the way for Mary. Apparent human impossibility meets divine possibility. The point of the earlier story is not the barrenness of Elizabeth but the extraordinary power of God; the point of this story, likewise, is not the virginity of Mary but an even greater illustration of that extraordinary power. But without doubt what gives this episode its potency is the way Luke weaves the supernatural and the natural. Luke's narrative skill threads the dialogue through with graceful ease. Divine invitation requires human response: 'God waits.' Luke's imagination allows this sacred space for contemplation, a time of waiting for the Word, first on Mary's part as she attends to the words of the angel and then on Gabriel's part as he waits for her word.

So we have Mary pondering, questioning, and finally accepting. And of course what is interesting here is that the message comes directly to Mary and not through Joseph. She is accorded respect and autonomy.

Fra Angelico, *The Annunciation* c.1438 (plate 2, page 54)

Artists frequently depict a rather passive virgin of the annunciation, but several demonstrate different emotions. Botticelli (1489) shows Mary rather gracefully holding her hands out as if to ward off what is coming. The angel holds up a hand suggesting reassurance. Simone Martini's famous painting, also in the Uffizi, shows the virgin backing away but being summoned by the angel Gabriel. The painter Lorenzo Lotto (1554-5) has one of the most dramatic annunciations of all – Mary turns away from the angel and towards the viewer with a startled expression and her hands raised as if to cry out 'No, no!' There is even a cat with its back arched in fright as the compelling and muscular angel kneels to deliver the message backed up by a bearded God the Father pointing to the hapless virgin. I have heard of, but not been able to trace, a Flemish painting where the change in atmosphere causes Mary to have a nose bleed!

I want to turn now to one of the classic depictions of the Annunciation: Fra Angelico's fresco in San Marco in Florence.

My journey of coming to re-cognise this painting, or perhaps to know it properly for the first time, has not been dissimilar to my experience with the scriptural text of the Annunciation. Reproductions of Fra Angelico's painting are prolific on convent walls and particularly in Dominican schools. They become so much part of the expected furnishings one does not see them any more. The over-familiarity of too often reproduced icons dulls their capacity to speak to us. The over-hyped Mona Lisa is a good example of this. Seeing it behind its bullet-proof glass is almost inevitably a disappointment.

On the other hand seeing Fra Angelico's 'Annunciation' 'in the flesh' as it were, for the first time did not disappoint.

San Marco in Florence is now a museum but houses its paintings and frescoes in the context for which they were created. The

Plate 2: *The Annunciation,* c.1438-45 (fresco) by Fra Angelico (Guido di
Pietro) (c.1387-1455). Museo di San Marco dell'Angelico, Florence,
Italy / www.bridgeman.co.uk

museum is part of a complex still used by the Dominican order.
So from the beginning we have a sense of sacred space. The
structure we see was created in the fifteenth century. On the
upper floor there are dormitories along three corridors and a
wonderful library.[38] Each cell is small but not cramped and has a
sense of simplicity and harmony. There is a narrow window to
allow light for reading and a small wooden door. To maintain
the sense of a community, there is a single beamed roof covering
the forty three cells. Starting in 1437 Fra Angelico, a member of
the order and an artist, started to paint frescoes for each of the
forty three cells with episodes from the life of Christ.

The pattern appears to have followed the sequence of birth-
passion, death-resurrection, corresponding to an abridged
rosary, in which to contemplate the principal joyful, sorrowful,
and glorious mysteries of the lives of Christ and the Virgin.
These were painted to enhance the private meditations of the
monks and were not known more widely until the secularis-
ation of the monasteries in 1869. Even now they retain that sense

of meditative stillness. Quite often the frescoes include Saint Dominic, sometimes with the Virgin. We see Dominic praying at the foot of the cross and at the nativity. Fra Angelico also presents an interesting interpretation of the Agony in the Garden, where we see Mary and Martha praying and 'staying awake' in contrast to the sleeping disciples. The praying saints in each case provide the model for the friars to follow. There is a sense of mystery as you enter each cell and discover its particular painting.

However the fresco which I want to focus on is the large Annunciation which was painted not for an individual cell but opposite the opening of the staircase linking the dormitories with the cloisters below. It was intended for all the friars to look on as they passed by – almost like a bell calling them to prayer. There is even an inscription to this end, 'Virginis intacte cum veneris ante figuram pretereundo cave ne sileatur Ave' (When entering and in front of the Virgin, take heed that you say an Ave.) Guidebooks describe how visitors turn on the staircase and when they catch their first glimpse are quite literally stopped in their tracks. I experienced this on my first visit on a bright January morning a few years ago. For about twenty minutes I stood alone and awed in front of this work. As I moved up the steps and closer to the fresco I could hear the break in the tread of later visitors as they too were held back. Even chattering school children were momentarily silenced.

One of the first things of which we become aware is the perspective of the painting. It is painted within what appears to be a window frame with its jambs, sill and lintel. You can almost feel the stone. You gaze through the window and there you see a loggia opening onto a garden full of flowers bordered by a slatted wooden fence behind which we see a further landscape. The architecture reflecting the work of Michelozzo on the floor below, and the small cell with its tiny window towards which the eye is drawn, all serve to make the mystery of the incarnation 'real and immediately present'.[40]

Light floods the interior space in which the virgin and the

angel meet. The light within the picture, created by the use of large quantities of white mixed with yellow, is enhanced by exterior light. So the first impression is of a radiant luminosity.

George Steiner, borrowing a phrase from the poet W. B. Yeats, uses the analogy of the Annunciation to describe the effect of an encounter with the aesthetic that is akin to certain modes of religious or metaphysical experience. He speaks of:

> 'a terrible beauty' or gravity breaking into the small house of our cautionary being. If we have heard rightly the wing-beat and provocation of that visit, the house is no longer habitable in quite the same way as before. A mastering intrusion has shifted the light (that is very precisely, non-mystically, the shift made visible in Fra Angelico's Annunciation).[41]

Making visible the shifting of the light is the effect of this painting. I am writing this on a brilliantly lit spring morning, where the dark rain-bearing clouds of the night before have given way to a day glorious with light. The incarnation floods the earth with light. John's gospel tells of this Light coming into the world; Luke mediates it through a divine/human encounter; Fra Angelico shows it.

After the effect of the light the next thing we notice is how each of the two figures occupies their separate spaces. The angel comes in from the left, the tip of the wonderfully rainbowed wing just hidden behind the first column, the other wing just touching the second pillar. This is Gabriel's space. He has come from the garden, but there is no sense of rush or urgency about this angel. His head is inclined towards the Virgin, his hands are folded across his breast, and he gazes directly, calmly, even reassuringly at the woman seated opposite him. His tunic falls in elegant folds to the ground, his knee, slightly bent, matches the incline of the head, and both reach towards but do not touch the pillar, which separates them from the Virgin. The messenger of God waits.

The Virgin is seated on a simple stool in front of her cell-like room. She also bends her head slightly forward as if considering what has just been said. She too exudes an air of profound calm.

Like the angel her gaze is direct and unflinching. She does not look away or raise her hands in horror; in fact in a gesture mirroring that of Gabriel, she folds them across her breast. The effect of the reflected gestures is to create a sense of utter harmony between the two figures. I imagine that when I passed this picture by on the school corridor, if I thought about it at all, I would have seen it as an image of humility, or at least of passivity. Now I see it differently: I see it as capturing a moment of contemplation, a moment pregnant with possibility. The painting transmits the calm and meditative presence that it portrays. The words of the archangel are significant, 'Salve Mater Pietatis et totius nobile Trinclinum' (Hail O Mother of mercy and noble Dwelling of the Holy Trinity). 'Mary is envisaged as an active and fully aware agent of redemption.'[42] This is a sophisticated theology of the incarnation – no visual image of a tiny infant hurtling towards the waiting virgin as we get in some depictions – here the mystery is expressed entirely through the delicate courteous stance of the two figures.

Commentators refer to the enclosed garden as a symbol for virginity, but what is less often observed is the sense of radical autonomy which is suggested in the careful separation of the spaces which the angel and the virgin occupy – and of course of utter importance, the space between them. The Virgin is not a passive vessel into which divine life is poured but a questioning, considering, reflective autonomous human person, engaged in a dialogue in which she is a partner. Here we do not see the hand of God the Father directing the action, or any visible sign of the Holy Spirit coming upon the Virgin, spiralling down as a dove, as in Fra Filippo Lippi's Annunciation;[43] we have nothing except the two figures and the space between them. It is daringly simple. It is utterly profound. I had thought of it as a visual image of 'call' and 'response' but now I think that it images the time of waiting. The angel waits. The virgin waits. The world stands still. As viewers, we too are held in this moment. We too hold our breath and as we breathe out again we become aware that the room is filled with light and that the woman is utterly present to what is happening and open to what it will mean. She knows that all has been 'changed utterly'. And so our eye is taken beyond the figures to and through the small cross-barred window at the back. As we look into the window which frames this picture we are called not merely to contemplate its mystery, but are also thrown back to our place in the drama of the incarnation which is made present now. Reducing the story to its essential elements, Fra Angelico takes the unique moment portrayed by Luke and gives it a universal significance. Allowing, indeed almost compelling, the viewer's response, it holds us too in a sacred space. We are caught in the same deep attentiveness to the moment. We too wait. Drawing in other senses I might compare it to the cleansing effect of listening to, or better singing, a piece of Gregorian chant. It centres us. It quiets us. The San Marco Annunciation fresco has become for me the quintessential Advent image. It embodies this time of stillness, this total attentiveness to the mystery, this utterly trustful waiting.

Plate 3: *The Visitation of St Elizabeth to the Virgin Mary* by
Mariotto Albertinelli (1474-1515)
Galleria degli Uffizi, Florence, Italy / www.bridgeman.co.uk

CHAPTER FOUR

The Journey: A Time of Letting Go

In those days Mary set out and went with haste to a Judean town and hill country ...

Countless artists have depicted the scene of the Annunciation and very many also show the Visitation, but few show the journey.[44] However, because I am interested in exploring the in-between spaces, the threshold places, the spaces between call and response, between fear and faith, between coming and going, I want to look now at this space between Annunciation and Visitation.

Journeys are always interesting. Consider the different moods on setting out and returning. There is something about being neither here nor there which is freeing. As one watches other travellers one quickly becomes aware of those for whom the journey is a necessary means to an end: they watch their clocks impatient of any delay, irritated by the crying infant in the seat behind, oblivious to the anxiety of the old lady taking her first flight to visit her dying sister in a far off country. There are others for whom the journey is part of the adventure. They come equipped with food and drink, books to read and stories to hear and share. Their eyes are eager as they search out the new experiences and across the carriage they proffer bread and grapes. Some are anxious; all their belongings gathered in untidy heaps among them, children clinging uncertainly to adults who are too preoccupied. Some are distressed; one woman's face is covered in bandages and she is led by another who smiles and reassures her. Some flee from 'Egypt', some from the contemporary sites of famine, war or disaster.

Then there are the stages in the journey, and that particular moment when one shifts from leaving to arriving, from going to coming, from ascending to descending, from taking off or setting out, to touching down, to coming in.

We can use journey time as a kind of letting go of what is behind us, to free us for what will come. Then coming back there is that slight anxiety that all the things we had hoped to let go of, are waiting in left luggage and will be too quickly picked up as we return. But something happens on the journey and they are never quite the same.

What happens on this, Mary's journey, which is marked by so few words? You could be quite prosaic and consider that it simply moves the action from one setting to another, but then you would miss 'the setting out' and the 'haste'. In order to know what it is to arrive, we need to reflect on the journey. 'Where have you come from? And where are you going?' the angel asked Hagar, and the questions have haunted us ever since.

Perhaps because we have had a tendency to sentimentalise the story of the Annunciation it might be salutary to set it alongside that painful and very different annunciation to Hagar as told in chapter sixteen of the book of Genesis. Mary may choose to describe herself as a 'slave of the Lord,' but Hagar is the slave of Sarah, wife of Abraham. She has no choice about her self-description. She has conceived a child through Abraham, and Sarah, jealous of her pregnancy, treats her harshly and Hagar flees. Her flight into the wilderness gives her a brief moment of autonomy but then she is sent back to further submit to Sarah. Her journey seems to have had no purpose. Yet in the wilderness the angel of the Lord also assured Hagar of innumerable descendants – a promise that usually comes to Patriarchs and not to slave girls – and confirms her pregnancy:

Now you have conceived and
shall bear a son;
and you shall call him Ishmael,
for the Lord has given heed to your affliction.

But this does not bring the absolute joy such news brought to Hannah. A longed-for pregnancy coming as a result of the love between two people is very different to a pregnancy which results from rape or coercion – 'Sarah took Hagar and gave her to her husband.'

This harsh reality is not mitigated by the promises which follow, particularly when Hagar is returned to her abusive situation. Phyllis Trible writing about this story gives it a resonance which we recognise: 'Suffering undercuts hope. A sword pierces Hagar's own soul.'[45] It provides a counterpoint in sorrow to the Annunciation to Mary.

However, we can acknowledge that Hagar is the first woman in the scriptures to receive an annunciation. There is however something more extraordinary than this: Hagar then proceeds to name the deity who has spoken to her, 'So she named the Lord who spoke to her, "You are El-roi," for she said, "Have I really seen God and remained alive after seeing him?"' 'You are a God of seeing' is what she says, becoming in that moment, as Trible points out, a theologian![46] The aspect that makes this encounter so arresting is the naming which connects the divine and the human. Hagar, like Mary, is not a passive recipient of this annunciation, but a participant in the drama of exchange.

Hagar is later banished by Sarah and Abraham and wanders in the wilderness, and when her supply of water has gone she fears that her child will die. The story tells us that God hears her cry – or that of her child – and opens her eyes to see a well. The boy survives and lives in the wilderness.

Yet we cannot consider that the story has a happy ending; its terror is too deep and it is still felt today. Trible describes the contemporary Hagar: 'She is the faithful maid exploited, the black woman used by the male and abused by the female of the ruling class, the surrogate mother, the resident alien without legal recourse ...'[47] She becomes every woman, cast out from their homeland because of war, or terror. The list could continue: she is the woman caught up in a conflict where she has no say and no power, she is a woman in a land devastated by famine, sucked dry by greed, she is a woman whose ethnic identity, whose religion, mark her as the despised other.

Why spoil our gentle tale of announcing angels and humble virgins with such a story? Feminist theologian Elisabeth Schüssler Fiorenza gives one reason:

> Sarah and Hagar symbolically prefigure the pitfalls and possibilities of a critical dialogue between Palestinian and European or American Christian women, between Christian, Jewish, and Muslim women living in the 'holy land' of biblical religions. This dialogue must first focus on the problematic relations exemplified in these two foremothers.

She argues that this relationship needs to be examined before we can rejoice in the coming together of Mary and Elizabeth, which is assumed to be a meeting in kinship. So the journey is hazardous. Recognising that might just begin to inhibit the tendency to tell the Christmas story as a 'spiritual fairy tale'.

So in the light of that harsher annunciation story let us return to the journey of Mary to her cousin. Viewed not from within a coherent symbol system or a faith-enriched telling, what we have is an unmarried, pregnant girl, possibly terrified, certainly anxious, setting out with haste to visit her cousin Elizabeth. As a school girl I recall being assured that Mary set out in order to offer assistance to her older cousin. In this case we may wonder why she left just prior to the birth. However, I have been fascinated to note how in almost every artistic depiction of the Visitation the reassurance comes not from Mary, but to her from Elizabeth. The young woman leaves her home pondering the strange encounter, wondering whether or not she imagined it all, but sure that what she feels happening inside is all too real. Before she shares this experience she needs somehow to come to terms with it. Luke's description of her response to the visit of the shepherds might apply equally well here: 'But Mary treasured all these words and pondered them in her heart.' The Greek word translated by 'pondering' is *symballo*, literally 'to throw together'; it is from this that the word 'symbol' comes. It seems appropriate to use it here. We are in unknown territory and, perhaps more than anything else, that is what is symbolised by this journey. Mary leaves what was once familiar, but by

Plate 4: George Mung Mung, *Mary of Warmun: The Pregnant Mary 1983*
By kind permission of Patrick Mung Mung

the time she returns, nothing will be as it was. The risk of 'yes' is now followed by the 'risk' of the journey. The poet Adrienne Rich captures this moment in her poem entitled: 'Prospective Immigrants Please Note':

> Either you will
> go through this door
> or you will not go through.
>
> If you go through
> there is always the risk
> of remembering your name.

The poet considers that it is of course possible not to go through and to 'live worthily', but the question is 'at what cost'? The poem concludes by reminding us that:

> The door itself
> makes no promises.
> It is only a door.[49]

Stepping out is a risk. The house is a shelter, another shell protecting us. We defend our territory and retreat there when threatened. We barricade it against the enemy, and even the stranger, with our gated entries, our coded doorways. Behind high walls we feel safe. Going forth is a risk. Leaving home is never easy, a constant replication of our birth journey. The gospels are full of invitations to leave the familiar and equally full of the hesitant responses: Let me first tend my cattle, feed my children, plant my crops ... In the Book of Ruth we often forget that there were two daughters-in-law, Orpah and Ruth. Both were told in no uncertain terms by Naomi to return to their 'mother's house'. They both protest and weep aloud and insist they will accompany Naomi, but as she argues with them and tells them that there is no future with her they weep once more and then 'Orpah kissed her mother-in-law but Ruth clung to her'. Because Ruth is the one who makes the journey we hear her story. Of Orpah who returns to her mother's house we hear nothing.

The journey which is taken at the beginning of the gospel of

Luke marks Mary out as a disciple. She is not caught in a paralysis of fear but goes out, knowing that nothing will ever be the same again. This stepping out into the unknown future follows immediately upon her assent to the divine word. This implies that waiting for the word is not a passive stance but an active commitment. This is of course expressed most fully in the *Magnificat*: 'He has brought down the powerful from their thrones, and lifted up the lowly'. For the moment though it is symbolised in the journey itself.

Paul Murray, in his book, *Journey with Jonah: The Spirituality of Bewilderment*, talks about the spiritual necessity of undergoing 'the grace and mystery of bewilderment':

> But, sometimes, it is only in the midst of a tempest, in the heart of a storm of circumstances which we can't control, that we come finally to realise something of the wonderful mystery of God.[50]

We can envisage the journey as such a time of bewilderment, a 'yes' has been voiced out of faith but now there is that shocked realisation of the consequences of that 'yes'. The journey exposes us to fears and to anxieties but as we continue moving forward, the knot of fear unravels and is replaced by trust. God is encountered, not just after the heart has ceased trembling, but in that trembling, not only in the calm which follows the storm, but in the storm itself.

God is encountered not only in the 'fiat' of Mary, but in her 'How can this be?' Letting go of all that is familiar she sets out.

CHAPTER FIVE:

The Encounter: A Time to Listen, A Time to Speak

Luke Chapter 1

... and she entered the house of Zechariah and greeted Elizabeth. When Elizabeth heard the greeting of Mary, the child leaped in her womb. And Elizabeth was filled with the Holy Spirit and exclaimed with a loud cry, 'Blessed are you among women, and blessed is the fruit of your womb. And why has this happened to me that the mother of my Lord comes to me? For as soon as I heard the sound of your greeting, the child in my womb leaped for joy. And blessed is she who believed that there would be a fulfilment of what was spoken to her by the Lord.'

And Mary said,

'My soul magnifies the Lord,

and my spirit rejoices in God my Saviour,

for he has looked with favour on the lowliness of his servant.

Surely from now on all generations will call me blessed;

for the Mighty One has done great things for me, and holy is his name.

His mercy is for those who fear him from generation to generation.

He has shown strength with his arm, he has scattered the proud in the thoughts of their hearts.

He has brought down the powerful from their thrones, and lifted up the lowly;

he has filled the hungry with good things, and sent the rich away empty.

He has helped his servant Israel, in remembrance of his mercy,

according to the promise he made to our ancestors, to Abraham and to his descendants for ever.'

And Mary remained with her about three months, and then returned to her home.

Let's change the focus for a moment from the one journeying
and arriving to the one expecting. Did messengers go on ahead
to prepare the way for this arrival? Was Elizabeth taken totally
by surprise? Did her surprise mirror that of her cousin's?

Remember Elizabeth has been in seclusion with a husband
struck dumb for six months now. A woman friend reflects on
how much she must have been longing for good conversation.
So we might expect that even before the child leaps in her
womb, her own heart stirs with joy. Later we will look at images
of the Visitation but for now I want to see what the words suggest, how we might imagine this encounter.

Mary greets Elizabeth, Elizabeth hears the greeting, the child
leaps in her womb, Elizabeth is filled with the Holy Spirit and
exclaims with a loud cry.

Notice how all the senses are engaged here: the women see
one another, Elizabeth then hears the voice of her cousin, the
child moves in the womb, and Elizabeth speaks. From the beginning this is an intensely bodily encounter. There could hardly be
a greater contrast with the meeting between the angel and Mary.
There all was distance and space, a sense of timelessness with
words like 'forever' and 'no end'. Words hovered in the air between the angel and the woman; there was talk of 'Holy Spirit',
'Most High Power' and 'overshadowing'. There was a tremu-
lous virgin, an ethereal messenger. The only thing grounding
the dialogue, shaping and framing it and finally rooting it was
the reference to the pregnancy of Elizabeth, 'in the sixth month',
'this is the sixth month'.

There is something solid about the sixth month; a pregnancy
is less vulnerable, more assured at that point. The bump is clearly
visible, the pregnancy cannot be hidden. On a recent visit to
Chartres Cathedral I noticed that there was one depiction of the
Visitation at one of the porches showing two tall slender women
their heads inclined towards one another. However a stone re-
lief inside the cathedral behind the altar showed a rather different image. Here there is a robust and round figure, a clearly
pregnant Elizabeth in voluminous clothes stretching a hand out

to Mary. You could almost hear her complaining of back pain or heartburn! As we shall see, artists almost without exception depict a thoroughly human encounter.

There is no doubt that words become flesh here. Three times the word 'womb' is repeated, 'her womb', 'your womb', 'my womb'. The wombs of women are the sites of revelation, and the sight of the swelling womb confirms the pregnancies. For Mary this visible sign of the invisible promise engenders trust. One might be mistaken about the fluttering of angel's wings but there is no mistaking the kicking of a child in the womb. Three mentions of 'womb,' two mentions of the leaping child and the mystery is earthed in the bodies of these pregnant cousins.

What is also so clear in both text and art is that Elizabeth is the one who offers support; she having received the grace of her pregnancy is now able to name the grace of this one. There is of course an ironic counterpoint here: Elizabeth rejoiced that 'disgrace' had been removed from her as the once barren woman became fertile; Mary must be concerned that her pregnancy will have the opposite effect and will be a cause of shame. The anxiety is unvoiced in Luke's gospel and is replaced by Elizabeth's reading of the situation. In a manner which anticipates the reversals of the gospel itself, Elizabeth immediately displaces any other possible perception by calling Mary 'blessed'. Elizabeth first names Mary herself as 'blessed among women' and after that blesses the 'fruit of your womb'. Then she refers the blessing or grace to herself, 'why has this happened to me ...' Then comes her understanding of what has happened, 'that the mother of my Lord comes to me.' This might conclude the address but there is more: Elizabeth tells of the child in the womb leaping for joy. And at that moment doubts are dispelled and the good news is made manifest. There is a final blessing for 'she who believed'.

If Elizabeth's pregnancy had provided the shelter, the holding space, in which the annunciation to Mary took place, here her words underline that role of support. Of course they also confirm her own status as a prophet. The mouth of Zechariah has been closed up and the mouths of the two women are opened to prophesy and to praise. From his muteness come their voices; out of his silence comes their speech. The house of Zechariah has become the domain of Elizabeth, she exercises the authority, she authors the script, and she gives the blessing. The house, and not the temple, has become the sacred space of blessings exchanged, of grace named, of singing out in exultation, of leaping for joy. In the words of Elizabeth Johnson, 'The outpouring of the Spirit on Elizabeth and Mary happens in a traditionally female domestic space.'[51] Elizabeth is the first person in the narrative to be described as 'filled with the Holy Spirit'; later we hear her proclaiming 'with a loud cry'. Her naming of Mary as 'mother of my Lord' almost passes unnoticed. Yet once again she confirms the words of the messenger Gabriel, but gives them the human twist of her own surprise and delight at the event.

Elizabeth's greeting releases the voice of Mary to sing out her song of exultation.

Mary picks up the tune from Hannah, the song-line from Miriam and lets them resound again and so God's mercy flows 'from generation to generation'. What is interesting about this song of liberation is that it does not express gratitude for the child but for God's gracious acts which reverse the fortunes of the poor: 'he has lifted up the lowly; he has filled the hungry with good things'. This is not a pious paean of praise but a subversive manifesto for the poor. Little wonder that it didn't form part of the traditional Marian devotions.

Elisabeth Schüssler Fiorenza quotes a dialogue from Latin America where the customary images of Mary dressed in blue and with a gold crown on her head are challenged by 'Mary of the Song':

The Mary of the song would not be standing on the moon. She would be standing in the dirt and dust where we stand. The Mary of the song would not be wearing a crown. She would have an old hat like the rest of us, to keep the sun from causing her to faint.[52]

To reimagine Mary in the light of this text is to see a young

Jewish peasant woman who proclaims a God of liberation. She refers to her 'lowliness' but this may simply be an objective statement of her situation which is now subject to transformation. She speaks as one empowered by the Spirit just as Elizabeth before her.

This is the other aspect which is so clear here and which again contradicts much traditional piety – the obvious solidarity between these women. They are depicted in dialogue together and although most manuscripts attribute the *Magnificat* to Mary, I like to imagine them singing together, with Elizabeth picking up the song where it moves from the particular 'for me', to widen out to include what God does for 'all who fear him'.

Pregnant women seek the support of one another. While writing this I came across a newspaper article detailing how contemporary women use the internet to share the anxieties and joys of pregnancy. The journalist referred to pregnancy as 'the biggest learning curve' in a woman's life. One of the women interviewed described how helpful she had found the site but then went on to say that she had organised a meeting with her on-line friends. They too met when they were six months pregnant – 'it was great to compare shapes!'[53] Pregnancy in itself demonstrates our interdependence so it is little surprise that women seek one another out to share this experience. At the very least this encounter is such a sharing, an exchange of wisdom, and a mutual support which helps Elizabeth through to the end of her pregnancy and enables Mary at the beginning of hers. Biblical commentators may have other interests and observe how this encounter enables the narrative or the literary structure, or how it underlines Luke's theological interests and how it bridges the gap between old Israel and New Israel. It may do all of these things but as a story, and read as such, it brings two women together in fear and in hope, in anxiety and in joy, in conversation, in consolation and in hope. Women can identify with this. They do it all the time. They know it is not good to be alone in these situations. They know that we are meant to be enablers of one another. They have no fear about seeking advice, about looking to the wisdom of the woman who has been there before them. They affirm one another. So Mary visits Elizabeth and the two women stand like sentinels at the beginning of salvation history, wise women of faith, wise women of the word. Women who know in the most bodily way possible, in the intimacy of their wombs, what it means for the word to take flesh.

The tradition has tended to focus on the one woman Mary but this fails to recognise the power of the solidarity with Elizabeth. It is of course potentially dangerous to speak of solidarity rather than sodality because, as other commentators have noted, these women do not seek validation from any male authority but rather look to one another. Pregnancy here becomes political. The *Magnificat* is a song of resistance. Every birth signals the capacity to begin again, to make things new; every birth is a word of hope. Mary is literally the bearer of 'the good news'; Elizabeth is the one who prepares her way as later John will prepare the way for Jesus. 'What emerges with undoubted clarity from their interaction is women's ability to interpret God's word for other women.'[54]

The *Magnificat*, the song of Mary, is described by Dietrich Bonhoeffer as 'the oldest Advent hymn':

It is at once the most passionate, the wildest, one might say the most revolutionary Advent hymn ever sung. This is not the gentle, tender, dreamy Mary whom we sometimes see in paintings; this is the passionate, surrendered, proud, enthusiastic Mary who speaks out here. This song has none of the sweet, nostalgic, or even playful tones of some of our Christmas carols. It is instead a hard, strong, inexorable song about collapsing thrones and humbled lords of this world, about the power of God and the powerlessness of humankind. These are the tones of the women prophets of the Old Testament that now come to life in Mary's mouth.[55]

The reversals proclaimed here are preached and lived out in the ministry of Jesus of Nazareth. A few years ago we were privileged in Dublin to see a production of *The Mysteries*, based on the Chester Mystery Plays which had originated in a South

African township and travelled to the West End of London, then visiting Dublin as part of a theatre festival. There is one scene where the beautifully round, even stocky Mary attempts to teach her son Jesus her song. At first he gets it wrong but she persists until he has learnt her song, until the rhythm has passed into his bloodstream, until he knows it by heart, then he in turn passes it on to his disciples. Mary's song may be sung by sweet-voiced boys and girls in cathedral choir stalls but its roots are with any people enslaved who hope for God's Advent, for God's saving mercy. The narrative of the visitation opens the space for Mary and Elizabeth to sing out their joy.

SEEING THE WORD

Albertinelli, *The Visitation of St Elizabeth to the Virgin Mary* (plate 3, page 59)

Does it show yet? Women ask one another anxiously or proudly as the case may be. The prurience which determined that pregnant women should conceal their pregnancy beneath voluminous clothing or behind closed doors has been replaced by a proud 'showing forth'. 'I love the way pregnant women walk' said a friend, 'with their eyes to the earth which they will soon populate!'

I have been fascinated by two things in particular as I have looked at images of the Visitation. The first and most striking thing is the sharp contrast with pictures of the Annunciation. In images of the Annunciation everything is distance, space, a formality of gesture, a convention of form and so on. In paintings of the Visitation the two figures seem to fill the given space, no room for lilies or prie-dieus, and no room for landscape or furnishings. Everything converges on the two women at their point of meeting which is invariably some form of embrace. In fact in the orthodox tradition *Aspasmos*, meaning embrace, is the title given to the scene. So where we had distance now we have closeness, where we had formality now we have intimacy, where we had angel's wings now we have flowing robes, where we had a pregnant pause, now we have two pregnant women.

The second point is in relation to those pregnancies. Sometimes there is a very clear 'showing' as if to demonstrate the fact of the incarnation. There is a painting in the Fogg Art Museum in Harvard by Richard Frueauf the Elder (c. 1455-1507) which shows each of the women in the same advanced stage of pregnancy.[56] Although the artist may have taken licence with the time his intent is clear. This is not a virtual but an actual pregnancy. It is a touching encounter in every sense of that word. The four hands meet and hold hands or arms in gestures which symbolise support and assurance. Both women have their eyes cast down as if looking either towards those helping hands or towards the swelling wombs. The expression on the older woman's face is calm and the younger woman mirrors that with perhaps the barest hint of anxiety. You could not describe this as 'a collision of joys' but rather as a meeting of assurance. There is a shadow on the ground, wing like in its shape, as if the announcing angel has just disappeared. Elizabeth stands in front of an arch; all is darkness behind, but light where the two women stand.

A contrasting image is that by Kathe Kollwitz. This is a contemporary etching produced in the first half of the last century. It is an immensely powerful depiction of the two women. We see an anxious almost anguished Mary with the older Elizabeth reaching out to whisper in her ear, to place an arm around her neck. Elizabeth's other hand rests on Mary's womb. Mary's hands hover as if she has just unfurled them from a tensed hold. She is not yet sure enough to return the embrace.

When showing images of the Visitation I always include this piece as I think that more than any other it challenges any romantic and sentimental reading. It subverts the pieties and questions the platitudes. Perhaps it is not surprising that I first encountered this image on the cover of a book by Elizabeth Schüssler Fiorenza, where she makes these very points.[57]

The fact that the two women are Jewish is also most apparent as is their poverty– both are thin, almost undernourished with hollowed cheekbones, so the work of art becomes more than an interpretation of a 'holy story' and expands to connect with contemporary concerns. We see a young refugee, we see a woman fleeing persecution, perhaps the victim of rape, we see a woman whose only hope is the solidarity and protection of this other woman who now holds her in her embrace, 'all will be well'. And if a woman in such a painful situation can be empowered through this meeting then it also gives enormous hope to all women.

To return to the 'showing' – the picture I have chosen to illustrate this text is by the Italian painter Albertinelli. Painted in 1503 it hangs in the Uffizi in Florence.

Once again Elizabeth reaches out to Mary. Her arm stretches to embrace her, her other hand clasps that of Mary. The younger woman in her dark cloak holds one hand up to her breast as if protecting a trembling heart. The expression on the face of the older woman is full of tenderness and reassurance. Her head is covered by a simple white cloth, frayed at the ends, catching the light; her cloak is beautifully rich in autumnal colours. She is one ready to bear fruit. As she leans towards Mary, the other woman inclines her head and upper body towards her cousin; the doubts are not yet entirely dispelled. However, unlike the Frueauf image, here the eyes meet. There the communion was in the hands; here it is through the eyes.

In each case the cloaks partly conceal and partly reveal, through their bulk, the pregnant shapes of the women. The clasped hands join the two women close to the swelling wombs.

They stand beneath a large arch which we see quite often in these paintings depicting the entrance through the womb into history.[58]

Elizabeth Jennings in her poem 'Visitation' imagines Mary's anxiety to share her secret as though 'telling would tame the terrifying moment'. She then describes the encounter:

And those two women in their quick embrace
Gazed at each other with looks undisturbed
By men or miracles. It was the child
Who laid his shadow on their afternoon
    By stirring suddenly, by bringing
Back the broad echoes of those beating wings.[59]

The meeting is an emotional one: here is someone who can understand and share this experience, who can help her make sense of it all, who can name the grace for her, who can bless her, embrace her, comfort and console her, it is all one; the human encounter mediates divine grace.

CHAPTER SIX

A Time of Waiting

Since the coming of Christ goes on forever – he is always he who is to come in the world and in the church – there is always an Advent going on. Jean Danielou[60]

I have always found endings difficult and maybe there is something appropriate in writing a book which concerns itself with 'a time of waiting' with 'the journey' with 'the pregnancy' and not with the arrival, and not with the birth. Advent itself has always looked beyond the actual birth of Jesus to touch into a longing for 'Christ to come again'. So perhaps it is fitting to stay with the notion of yearning and longing, of waiting for the Word which speaks us into life. Without this forward thrust there may be a danger of settling for the givens or giving up on our desires, assuming that the last word has been spoken, when in our hearts the first word has not yet been heard.

A friend produced a book of fairy tales by contemporary Swiss writers. One tale told the story of a giraffe who wished for a long, slender neck. 'But,' said the little bird who lived on her back, 'You already have a long slender neck', 'That doesn't matter,' replied the giraffe, 'I can't get rid of the wish.' This seemed to me a wonderful summary of the human condition, we are a people who 'can't get rid of the wish'.[61]

Consider the huge pressure of consumerism at Christmas time. We are encouraged to wish for things and then we receive them beautifully, tastefully, gaudily packaged. We try to conceal it but we know as soon as we open the gift there will be an inevitable sense of disappointment. 'Is that it?' the small child asks when all the presents have been unwrapped. The wish remains even if you get what you asked for, especially if you get what you asked for! The longing is unsatisfied.

George Herbert understood this. He imagines God with a glass of blessings, pouring them out on the created human person: strength, beauty, wisdom, honour, but then God holds back 'rest'. And in typically Herbert fashion playing on the double meaning, he says that 'man' may keep 'the rest' of the gifts,

'Yet let him keep the rest,
But keep them with repining restlessness;
Let him be rich and weary, that at last
If goodness lead him not, yet weariness
    May toss him to my breast.'[62]

Rowan Williams, in a sermon written for Advent, considers the gap between Advent longing and the reality of God:

Advent insists that we stay for a while in this tension of being 'on the eve', if only in order that the new thing we celebrate at Christmas may have a chance of being truly new for us ... The Advent tension is a way of learning again that God is God; that between even our deepest and holiest longing and the reality of God, is a gap which only grace can cross.[63]

Williams speaks of the dangers of idolatry, echoing Elisabeth Schüssler Fiorenza's fear of spiritual consumerism which does not dislodge but reinforces 'the cultural fairy tale of Christmas'. Yet she too would argue that even commercialisation has not been able 'to eradicate their revolutionary power of transformation.'[64] Williams insists that Advent is the time when we all become Jews once more:

We relearn the lessons of the first covenant: that we cannot make God ... that we must be surprised, ambushed and carried off by God if we are to be kept from idols.[65]

Because I am interested in this time of waiting, this time of being 'on the eve', of longing for wisdom, of expecting, of journeying hopefully, I see this yearning as reaching beyond the particular liturgical season of Advent and addressing the universal longing for God who is to come.

In that sense this longing cannot cease at Christmas or any other time until we die into truth. And so we can answer the child, 'No, that's not it', 'No, that's not all there is.' 'And you won't get rid of the wish.' Perhaps much later the child will learn the lesson of Augustine and come to know that there is a space inside us that nothing but the uncontained God can fill. The restlessness will lead at last to rest.

Yet I don't want to move into abstractions here because this waiting is not simply for 'a word' but for 'the word made flesh' and it is in that human reality that it touches us, speaks to us, and addresses us. It is surely no accident that the images used in this book have almost all been images of relationship, of communication, and two indeed of embrace. There is no image of a solo figure. And the one I have chosen to discuss next will demonstrate in a most explicit way the word taking flesh, *Mary of Warmun* or *The Pregnant Mary* (Plate 4, page 64).

Before I come to that I want to look again briefly at the spaces we marked along the way. Perhaps we could revisit them, seeing them as spaces cleared for the possibility of revelation, places open for the surprise of grace. This time I want to translate those images into contemporary experience.

Barrenness and Expectancy

Pregnancy is a potent symbol, whether or not we have had that actual experience – and by definition half of the human race has not. Writers and artists know about the period of gestation before something new comes to birth. All of us recognise that sense of labouring painfully to bring something forth. Saint Paul in his letter to the Romans drew on such images, 'For creation waits with eager longing for the revealing of the children of God ... We know that the whole creation has been groaning in labour pains until now; and not only the whole creation but we ourselves.'

However, there is a condition prior to pregnancy which scripture also recognises and provides many stories to illustrate, and that is the condition of barrenness. We looked at this in relation to both Hannah and Elizabeth. Barrenness was used to demonstrate the gratuitousness of the gift of birth. But here I want to consider it as a state common to all our experience.

A Jungian writer Joy Ryan-Bloore comments:
Psychologically barrenness means that the old way, the old
order doesn't bear fruit any more. And the new order is yet
to evolve ... Barrenness also means emptiness and therefore
a state of potential receptivity.[66]

Many women and men go through times when their spiritual
and religious life feels barren. The old symbols and traditions no
longer resonate, the wells have dried up and yet they fear to go
elsewhere. They may be afraid to voice this anxiety but a nag-
ging pain gnaws at them. The Hannah story offered some help.
Elkanah, her husband, tries to deal with pain by consoling her,
'Am I not more to you than seven sons?' he asks as he offers her
an extra portion. But Hannah knows that consolation for this
state is found neither in the distractions of gifts, nor even in
other people. She must look to her own soul. We saw how her
whole body became a prayer of longing, how her distress was
too deep for any words, and how her crying out became the
moment of transformation. It was then that the emptiness became
a space filled with yearning. Desire replaced bitterness and she
was open again to be touched and called back to life, to hope.
The barren landscapes of the culture of the soul seem to mirror
the biblical wilderness awaiting an awakening voice to call them
into life again. But first they must be lamented. Hannah's crying
out in her wilderness precedes that of John the Baptist.

While writing this piece I happened to see a quirky small film
called *The Station Agent*.[67] Set in rural New Jersey it tells the
story of Finn – let us simply say he is a dwarf and lay aside the
sanitised political correctness which does not diminish anyone's
pain, nor increase his small stature by one iota. When Finn's
business partner, who is also his friend, dies suddenly, he leaves
Finn a disused railway and station master's house. Finn retreats
there determined to lead a solitary life. His one interest is train-
spotting. He has learnt to build a wall around himself and appears inured to finding himself the butt of the inevitable and
repetitive jokes, 'Where's snow-white etc.?', and the casual cru-
elties which are daily events. His face barely registers a flicker of

irritation let alone anger or pain when, for example, a woman in a shop takes out her camera to photograph him, or an assistant says, yet again, 'Sorry I didn't see you.' In his new home he encounters the ebullient Hispanic Joe who runs a snack bar and yearns for company with the same intensity with which Finn rejects it. He pursues Finn and is joined by Olivia, an artist mourning the death of her child. At first Finn's protective shell will not allow of any intrusion but he is worn down by Joe and gradually accepts the companionship. However, when Olivia, going through her own crisis, backs away and rejects Finn, and when Joe fails to show up as promised to meet him for a drink, Finn becomes angry. Sitting in the bar alone he gets drunk, stands on the table and cries out, 'Just take a good look, just look at me, that's you want to do isn't it?'

He leaves and staggers down the railway line. We see a train approaching and fear for him, but when the train passes Finn gets up, he is alive, it is simply his stop watch which has smashed. From this moment where the wound has been exposed, where Finn has cried out his pain, there is the possibility of transformation and the grace of healing. The friends regroup but on a different and deeper level having confronted their vulnerable selves.

I find in this completely secular story a deep humanity, a contemporary parable, a journey through barrenness and into birth – and not a pregnant woman in sight! This tale of moving out of the wilderness and into a space where growth is possible – an irony which Finn would enjoy – is a painful process. It brings terror as well as joy. It is safer as Finn knows to stay locked in, to remain protected where nothing can hurt us any more. In such a place there is no yearning. Waiting for trains and timing them is a less risky exercise than waiting for human beings on whom we come to depend but who may call us out of ourselves and bring us to life again. Symbolically the smashing of the watch signals the end of that phase of controlling time and opens Finn to a new space where he can be surprised by the grace of friendship. The film is punctuated by the sharing of meals and also by the rejection of offers of food and drink symbolising the state of the relationships.

Sacred Spaces

The awakened soul, the awakened capacity to receive when the period in the wilderness is over, is demonstrated in different ways by Mary and Elizabeth. Elizabeth's rejoicing is clear as it follows her time of suffering but she has not descended so far into the darkness as not to be able to recognise grace when it falls on her. The scene with Mary is rather different; there is no prelude; there is no preparation for this kind of shocking awakening. But what interested me in the story and where we paused to reflect was the in-between space, the space to which we were alerted by the Fra Angelico painting, the space between call and response. I have long been intrigued by Simone Weil's description of religion as 'attention animated by desire'. We see that quality of attention in small children – but they quickly lose it – and this is not surprising. Watch a small child fascinated by a snail making its slimy track along the path, or two flies on a window pane, a spider in a web or even their own reflection caught with a rainbow in a puddle of water. Hear the accompanying adult cry 'Come on, come on' and their concentration is broken and the capacity for deep attention is unlearnt to be supplanted by the fleeting attention demanded by the television screen. The capacity for 'seeing things' becomes a rarity practised later only by artists and poets. And what we have lost we seek again by turning to them with our cry, 'give us a vision', 'let us see again', as urgently as any blind beggar in the gospels.

I seem to have strayed from 'the Annunciation' but I wanted to connect this story with the little annunciations which happen in all our lives when our attention is focused, when our waiting is unforced, when a space is cleared and opens to reveal new possibility to us. We tend to imagine those moments of revelation taking place in still places, in the apparently sacred spaces of churches and cathedrals. The contemplative monk, Thomas Merton, describes such a moment occurring in 'Louisville, at the corner of Fourth and Walnut, in the centre of the shopping district'. In that place he is overwhelmed by the realisation of love connecting all of these people, he discovers that it is a 'glorious destiny to be part of the human race ... a member of a race in which God himself became incarnate.'[68] There is nothing in this of 'muscular effort' as Simone Weil says, it comes unbidden, sometimes unwanted, it catches us unawares and we are overwhelmed.

The call which awakens the self is imaged as an angel in Luke's version, an angel called Gabriel – Eckhart, rather endearingly I think, argues that his name could just as well have been Conrad! In other words the name is not significant. What matters is that the artist Luke, like Fra Angelico in a different medium, attempts to translate this moment so that we can grasp it. Now we try once more to translate their work into a contemporary idiom so that we too can grasp it, can see it, can in turn be grasped by it, can be seen, and can be awakened from our habitual slumber. We are reminded again of the Levertov poem, 'Aren't there annunciations/of one sort or another/in all our lives?'[69]

The space painted by Fra Angelico between the breathing out of the word of the angel and the breathing in of Mary, is a sacred space, and we recognise it. We know that moment of holding our breath. We've done it watching the light on the water just before the sun sets, or watching a flock of geese fly in at sunrise, and then we let out an 'Ah!' of wonder.

Denise Levertov talks about how days pass when she forgets the mystery, she describes how problems jostle for her attention like courtiers with 'cap and bells'.

Then 'once more the quiet mystery/is present to me ...'

In 'The Annunciation' as shown by Fra Angelico the 'quiet mystery' is made present again to us. Our own attention is animated again and we too become more aware, the scales fall from our eyes and we see.

Here and There
The next space we marked was that of the journey which opened a distance between 'here' and 'there'. We spoke about the symbolic nature of all our journeys, all our setting out. We acknowl-

edged the desire to retreat, the struggle to let go of the familiar, the fears which accompany any coming out. In *The Station Agent*, although Finn is an expert on trains, he doesn't appear to travel in them, and instead we see him walking the tracks towards his new destination. As he leaves the city carrying a suitcase he makes his solitary journey, each step putting distance between him and the past. Walking requires a physical effort; it has the pace of pilgrimage. Of course what we often don't bargain for is that the things we seek to leave behind have a habit of travelling with us and insisting on being our companions. This is of course particularly true in the case of our fears; our shadow goes with us.

Until Finn turns to face all the pain that he has avoided, no matter how much track he covers, his journey will not bring him anywhere.

Meetings and Midwives

The place of meeting, the Visitation, which of course is not a final resting place but a stop along the way, demands no particular skills of the translator. The images need no mediator – they are immediate. Hovering words take flesh in the embrace of the two women. I found myself thinking of other places of encounter. Airports are not the most pleasant places to be but I quite like the arrivals hall – it offers a concentration of meetings! You watch the people come through, the men and women on business flights carry only a briefcase and give a brief glance to see if their taxi is there and are gone. Others come out, their eyes anxiously scanning the row for a familiar face. When they recognise someone the expression changes, bags are dropped, arms held out. On one occasion a whole family gathered carrying placards to welcome home a baby adopted from China. Suddenly we all seemed to become part of the wave of warmth settling on this new arrival. A mother waits anxiously for a daughter who has been away for a year. Will she have changed? She will, and what is visible will be the least of it. There is a young man, he knows no one, and probably doesn't know much of the language either, but he looks about to see if he can find reassurance in any of the watching eyes. There is a young girl, she is pregnant and anxious. Her cousin is waiting to meet her. She wonders what her response will be. When she hears the warmth in her cousin's voice, tears fill her eyes and she rejoices. The full story will come with the unpacking of the bags.

No, we don't need translators to mediate these exchanges. We can identify with the experience of longing and hope that is in the eyes of the ones arriving, their searching out of one who will hear what they have to say. The greeting may be followed by weeping, as well as joy but for a moment the anxieties are held back and prodigal sons and daughters are fulsomely embraced.

The two waiting women have found their wisdom in one another; they have discovered it in their own bodily experience. It has come to life in them. They have needed one another to bring it forth. Elizabeth not only bears the word herself but is midwife to the Word in Mary. This is hugely encouraging and not just for women.

Which of us has not been consoled simply by finding someone who will truly listen to what we need to say? Which of us has not rejoiced in the experience of finding someone whose voice names something for us, for which we had no words but only the unarticulated longing? Which of us has not rejoiced in finding someone whose encouragement has enabled us to find our own voice? Perhaps that encounter is even more profound; at its heart is total acceptance of the other. One arrives carrying what she perceives to be a burden; she leaves bearing a gift. The facts of the situation have not changed but her perception of them is radically altered. From the hesitant beginning comes the song at the end.

Word-bearers

There is so much excitement when a child speaks its first words. The word 'infant' which we use to describe the new-born, in its Latin origin *infans*, means 'without speech'. So we hold the child, we caress the child and constantly we talk to and sing to the child, until the child – who first has listened – is led into speech, and becomes herself a word-bearer and this is the oldest term in the English language for a human being, 'reord-berend,' word-bearer.[71]

And there will follow wondrously the capacity to play, and to play with words, to reach beyond what is given, and to imagine, to be makers of symbols: creators of art and music (some will lose this and have no memory of their capacity; others will live by their art). The child will hear stories again and again and will learn to tell them. And the child will learn that the word is not fixed, it is not a dead letter, but a dancing, creative, living presence, a Word waiting to become flesh in her.

SEEING THE WORD

George Mung Mung, *Mary of Warmun: The Pregnant Mary 1983* (plate 4, page 64)

So as the final image, I have chosen such a 'dancing creative presence': *Mary of Warmun* or *The Pregnant Mary*. There is a wonderful contrast between the stillness of the Fra Angelico and the liveliness of this image. This is an aboriginal sculpture brought to public attention by the Australian art historian Rosemary Crumlin.[72] She tells the story of how the artist George Mung Mung cut the wood from a tree in the remote Bungle Bungle Ranges of Western Australia.

The purpose was to create an image of Mary which would not break as the old plaster image had been knocked over by dogs. I found myself thinking of the symbolism of that process: the plaster images of blue and white virgins no longer speak to our culture either and our task is similar to that of this artist – to create an image that will speak again to us.

Mung Mung has worked in such a way as to be faithful both to his Aboriginal roots and to his Catholic beliefs in Mary as the Mother of Jesus and in the incarnation.

The figure shows an unmarried Warmun girl; her body is painted with traditional designs. She is pregnant and carries the child in the 'womb-shield' beneath her heart.

Although it is Elizabeth who speaks of the child leaping in her womb, here the child dances in the womb of Mary. The child stretches out touching each corner of the womb as if inhabiting a total cosmos, 'I'm ready to be born.' It was this dancing lively image which so appealed to me. There is a quiet solemnity on the face of the expectant mother as she holds her arms protectively around the womb. But the child dances and the eyes are bright and open. The image challenges us with its startling dissimilarity to traditional images of Mary. It awakens our capacity to reimagine the word made flesh. It portrays in an utterly simple and yet profound way the notion of being as being-in-relationship. The arms of Mary form a circle around the egg shaped womb. New life is protected, but when it is ready it will be released into the world.

An Anglican priest John Waterhouse mused on how it was possible that:

> ... a bit of an old tree branch ... shaped with a sharpened car spring has become for me the most powerful evocative spiritual image I know? ... The fact of Mary as the mother of Jesus is overwhelming and I think it was the realisation of the physicality of the incarnation – God being carried in the womb of a young girl – that stunned me.[73]

Once again I want to connect the two apparently utterly different images: the Fra Angelico Annunciation and the George Mung Mung. Both were created for their particular communities, both were formed out of a deep and profound religious sensibility. Neither work belongs in an art gallery, but to a people, to a place with a living tradition. Both convey an extraordinary sense of presence. In the first there is that deep sense of waiting for the Word, in the second we see the Word made flesh in the womb of Mary. We see her continued calm, serene presence, but this time we also see the leaping dancing child, Wisdom's child — waiting to be born.

Epilogue

I wait for the Lord, my soul waits,
and in his word I hope;
more than those who watch for the morning,
more than those who watch for the morning.
Psalm 130

Eliot's Magi came for a birth and there certainly was one, but it also felt like death.[74] What they thought were so different – birth and death – appeared the same. The artist Bellini painted a scene called *The Madonna of the Meadows* showing the infant Jesus slumbering in his mother's arms against the backdrop of a landscape. But something seems a little disturbing about the image. On closer glance the pallor of the child appears unnatural, he is white as death and his limbs seem stiff. The mother has her hands closed in prayer rather than around her child; a raven sits in a bare tree. With a slight shiver we realise that we are observing a Pietà. Indeed Bellini painted a similar picture but this time of an aged virgin – unusual in itself – and a fully grown Christ lying dead across her lap. In this case we notice that the tree to the left of the picture has been cut down, but from the trunk new shoots sprout.[75] Where we expect only the joy of birth there are signs of death; where we expect only death there are signs of life.

There is the first breath, and the last rasp and in-between the thread of breath pulls us through our life-span. It may seem strange to conclude a book about 'A Time of Waiting', an Advent theme anticipating birth, with a 'Time of Waiting' which anticipates death. 'And how are you?' the young woman asks the elderly man; 'Waiting to die', he answers. Her instinct is to contradict him, to seek to 'jolly him along', his expression silences her protest. That she may not be ready to hear this is her problem and not his. She is the pupil here. If she waits with him he may teach her how to die. At this moment she is afraid and

88

hurries out of the nursing home and into the sunshine.

Having given birth to three children and watched the won-drous fragility of the first breath grow in strength to the full cry which signals life, and then more recently having watched my parents draw their last labouring breaths and die, I have seen the circle close. In between we danced at weddings. Now I go to the funerals of the friends of my parents or the parents of my friends. Both birth and death were accompanied by watchers. One of my children was born at midday, my mother died at that time of day; another child was born at first light and bears a name to prove it; my father died as 'dawn was breaking'. In the first cases labour was followed by joy, in the second, labour was followed by sorrow. In the first a space was filled with a new presence, in the second a space was emptied by a new absence. So where is this similarity? What feels the same? Is it the hard labour that accompanies both? Is it the sense of a long journey being completed – the journey of ascent, the journey of descent? We speak of women 'giving birth', we are born. But no one 'gives death' and if they do, we name it differently; to be killed is not the same as to die. We are carried to our birth and in one of the most beautiful images from Isaiah the prophet imagines God as the mother, who having carried us from the womb, also car-ries us to our death:

> Listen to me, O house of Jacob,
> All the remnant of the house of Israel,
> Who have been borne by me from your birth,
> Carried from the womb;
> Even to your old age I am she,[3]
> Even when you turn gray I will
> Carry you.
> I have made, and I will bear;
> I will carry and will save.

We are back to the concept of waiting in trust. On the cover of this book there is a detail from a painting by Fra Angelico which is a sublime rendering of trustful waiting. More than any other this image seemed to evoke this immensely powerful sense of total attentiveness, complete trust, a profound sense that indeed 'All things will be well'. The line is often cited and we may think of Julian of Norwich basking in heavenly peace, and indeed feel the same about the image of the waiting Virgin. Yet Julian's sense of trust came only after a considerable struggle. Such confidence – and that word itself holds *fides*, faith – is born out of hard thinking and suffering. She writes:

> ... deeds are done that appear so evil to us and people suffer such terrible evils that it does not seem as though any good will ever come of them; and we consider this, sorrowing and grieving over it so that we cannot find peace in the blessed contemplation of God as we should do ... And this is what he means when he says, 'You shall see for yourself that all manner of things shall be well', as if he said, 'Pay attention to this now, faithfully and confidently, and at the end of time you will truly see it in the fullness of joy.'[4]

This is no cheap grace but the grace that comes paradoxically not because 'all is well' but perhaps the very opposite: out of disorder and chaos grace shall be wrought. Our waiting is in vain if we are looking for that time of peace and tranquillity before we begin to trust, before we begin to pray. Julian seems to say that we should pay attention to the things around us but all the time trusting that there is ultimately a meaning and wisdom beyond our present comprehension.

This is the fundamental distinction between optimism and hope: optimism looks on the bright side; hope sees the dark light of the cross, the shadow of death yet fears no ill. Optimism can easily be shattered by bad luck, by misfortune; hope tenaciously holds on and because it is linked with faith, and with desire, it insists that good will prevail. Hope is an active searching out of this good. Hope is alert. Hope keeps watch.

The psalmist talks of a waiting and a hope which is more than watching for the morning, it is a waiting and watching in the darkness, until there is a dying into light, until there is a birth.

Advent.

Notes

1. Patrick Kavanagh, 'Advent' in *Collected Poems*, Martin Brian & O'Keefe, London 1972, page70.

2. Timothy Radcliffe OP, *Sing A New Song: The Christian Vocation*, Dominican Publications, Dublin 1999, page 184.

3. As a useful resource for Advent and details of these carols, see *Advent for Choirs*, compiled and edited by Malcolm Archer and Stephen Cleobury, Oxford, Oxford University Press 2000.

4. Rowan Williams, *Silence and Honey Cakes: TheWisdom of the Desert*, Lion Publishing, Oxford 2003, page 76.

5. Neil MacGregor, *Introductiohn to the Image of Christ: The Catalogue of the exhibition Seeing Salvation*, National Gallery Company Limited, London 2000, page 7.

6. Ibid, page 7.

7. George Herbert, 'Prayer' in *The Metaphysical Poets* introduced and edited by Helen Gardner, Penguin Books 1967, page 124.

8. Paul Tillich, *The Shaking of Foundations*, 1948. Cited in *Advent: An Advent Sourcebook* edited by Thomas J. O'Gorman, Liturgy Training Publications, Chicago 1998, page 5.

9. *Babette's Feast* directed by Gabriel Axel, 1987, based on a short story by Isak Dinesen.

10. Tom Hodgkinson, 'Branded for Life', a review of *Willing Slaves: How the Overwork Culture is Ruling Our Lives*, by Madeleine Bunting, HarperCollins 2004, in *The Guardian Review* 03.07.04, page 9.

11. Rowan Williams, *Silence and Honey Cakes*, pages 72, 73.

12. Genesis 4:20

13. Genesis 18:12

14. Walter Brueggemann, *The Bible and the Postmodern Imagination*, SCM Press London, 1993, page 30.

15. Ibid, page 31.

16. Psalm 104:29

17. Psalm 139:13, 14

18. Kathleen Norris, 'Advent' in *Cries of the Spirit* edited by Marilyn Sewell, Beacon Press, Boston 1981, page 63.

19. Adrienne Rich, 'The Spirit of Place' in *The Fact of a Doorframe, Selected Poems 1950-2001*, W.W. Norton & Company, New York London 2002, page 185.

20. Denise Levertov, 'Variation and Reflection on a Theme by Rilke' in *Breathing the Water*, Bloodaxe Books, Newcastle upon Tyne 1988, page 76.

21. Adrienne Rich, 'Integrity' in *The Fact of a Doorframe: Selected Poems 1950-2001*, W. W. Norton & Company New York London 2002, pages 171-172.

22. The story of Hannah is told in the book of Samuel Chapter 1:1-28; and Chapter 2:1-10 (Hannah's song).

23. Exodus 6:23

24. The story of Elizabeth is told in the gospel of Luke, Chapter 1, verses 5-80.

25. Barbara Reid, *Choosing the Better Part: Women in the Gospel of Luke*, The Liturgical Press, Minnesota 1996, page 60.

26. Herbert McCabe OP, *God, Christ and Us*, edited with an introduction by Brian Davies OP, Continuum, London and New York, 2003, page 1.

27. Ibid, page 8.

28. *The Oxford Companion to Christian Art and Architecture*, compiled by Peter and Linda Murray, Oxford University Press, Oxford/New York 1996, page 198.

29. For a discussion on these points see David Ford, *Self and Salvation, Being Transformed*, Cambridge University Press, Cambridge 1999, pages 191-215.

30. See Phyllis Trible, *God and the Rhetoric of Sexuality*, SCM Press London 1992.

31. Ibid, page 144.

32. *Meister Eckhart: Selected Writings*, Penguin Books London 1994, Sermon 2 (DW 38, W29), page 112.

33. Charles Causley, 'Ballad of the Breadman', in *Collected Poems 1951-1975*, Papermac Macmillan London 1983, pages 165-167.

34. Denise Levertov, 'Annunciation' in *A Door in the Hive, Evening Train*, Bloodaxe Books Ltd., Newcastle onTyne 1993, page 87.

35. John Drury, *Painting the Word: Christian Pictures and their Meaning*, Yale University Press, New Haven and London in association with National Gallery Publications Limited London, 1999, page 41.

36. Elizabeth Johnson, *Truly Our Sister: A Theology of Mary in the Communion of Saints*, Continuum, New York, 2003, pages 253, 254.

37. 'Ballad of the Breadman', page 165.

38. For detailed descriptions of San Marco and its frescoes the following works are useful: Giovanna Damiani, *San Marco Florence: The Museum and its Art*, Philip Wilson Publishers Limited, London 1997, and in particular, Paolo Morachiello, *Fra Angelico: The San Marco Frescoes*, Thames and Hudson London, 1996.

39. Paolo Morachiello, *Fra Angelico: The San Marco Frescoes*, page 43. This superbly illustrated volume provides details of the complete fresco cycle, with valuable introductory articles.

40. Ibid, page 269. I have drawn on the detailed description of the painting provided here.

41. George Steiner, *Real Presences*, Faber and Faber Limited, London 1989, page 143.

42. Paolo Morachiello, *Fra Angelico: The San Marco Frescoes*, page 270.

43. National Gallery London, late 1450s.

44. There is one wonderful 'Walking Madonna' by Elizabeth Frink outside Salisbury Cathedral in England, but it depicts Mary as an older woman in a post-resurrection period. It is however a compelling contemporary vision of Mary as a woman of compassion walking among her people.

45. Phyllis Trible, *Texts of Terror: Literary-Feminist Readings of Biblical Narratives*, SCM Press Ltd 1992, page 17.

46. Ibid, page 18.

47. Ibid, page 28.

48. Elisabeth Schüssler Fiorenza, *Jesus: Miriam's Child, Sophia's Prophet*, SCM Press Ltd 1994.

49. Adrienne Rich, 'Prospective Immigrants Please Note' in *The Fact of a Doorframe: Selected Poems 1950-2001*, pages 24, 25.

50. Paul Murray OP, *A Journey with Jonah: The Spirituality of Bewilderment*, The Columba Press, Dublin 2002, page 61.

51. Elizabeth Johnson, *Truly Our Sister*, page 259.

52. Robert McAfee Brown, *Theology in a New Key: Responding to Liberation Themes*, Westminster Press, Philadelphia 1978, pages 99-100. Cited in Elisabeth Schüssler Fiorenza, *Jesus: Miriam's Child, Sophia's Prophet*, pages 181, 182.

53. *The Irish Times*, Health Supplement, 'Going on-line with a bump', February 24 2004, page 3.

54. Elizabeth Johnson, *Truly Our Sister*, page 263.

55. Sermon preached by Dietrich Bonhoeffer on the Third Sunday of Advent ,1933. Cited in Elizabeth Johnson, *Truly Our Sister*, page 267.

56. Reproduced with commentary in Richard Harries, *A Gallery of Reflections: The Nativity of Christ*, Lion Publishing, The Bible Reading Fellowship, Oxford 1995.

57. Elisabeth Schüssler Fiorenza, *Jesus: Miriam's Child, Sophia's Prophet*.

58. Sister Wendy Beckett, *Sister Wendy's 1,000 Masterpieces*, Dorling Kindersley, London 1999, page 6.

59. Elizabeth Jennings, 'The Visitation', *Collected Poems*, Carcanet Press, Manchester and New York 1987, page 46.

60. From Jean Danielou, *The Advent of Salvation*, cited in *An Advent Sourcebook*, page 159.

61. Max Huwyler, 'Geschichte mit Tieren drin', in Gabrielle Alioth, *Ach wie gut dass niemand weiss: Ein Schweizer Lese-und Vorlesebuch*, Nagel & Kimche, 2004.

62. George Herbert, 'The Pulley' in *The Metaphysical Poets*, edited by Helen Gardner, Penguin Books Limited London 1967.

63. Rowan Williams, *Open To Judgement: Sermons and Addresses*, Darton, Longman and Todd, London, 1994, pages 10, 11.

64. Elisabeth Schüssler Fiorenza, *Jesus: Miriam's Child, Sophia's Prophet*, page 185.

65. Rowan Williams, *Open to Judgement*, page 10.

66. From a series of addresses given for Advent 2003 in Melbourne Australia (by permission of the author).

67. Directed by Tom McCarthy 2003.

68. Thomas Merton, 'At the Corner of Fourth and Walnut' cited in *Something Understood, A Spiritual Anthology*, edited by Sean Dunne, Marino Books, Dublin 1995, page 48.

69. Denise Levertov, *A Door in the Hive*, page 87.

70. Denise Levertov, 'Primary Wonder' in *Sands of the Well*, Bloodaxe Books, Newcastle upon Tyne 1998, page 129.

71. For these insights I am indebted to Malcolm Guite, 'Through Literature: Christ and the Redemption of Language' in *Beholding the Glory: Incarnation Through the Arts*, edited by Jeremy Begbie, Darton Longman and Todd, London 2000, pages 33, 34.

72. I am indebted to Rosemary Crumlin for introducing me to this work. The comments which follow draw on her description of the image in: Rosemary Crumlin, *Beyond Belief: Modern Art and the Religious Imagination*, National Gallery of Victoria, Melbourne 1998.

73. John Waterhouse, 'Divine humanity in a bit of old branch' http://www.media.anglican.com.au/tma/2003/08/mary.html

74. T. S. Eliot, 'Journey of the Magi', *The Complete Poems and Plays*, Faber and Faber, London and Boston 1969, pages 103, 104.

75. *The Image of Christ: The catalogue of the exhibition Seeing Salvation*, Gabriele Finaldi, National Gallery Company Limited, London 2000, page 62.

76. The verses come from Isaiah 46:3-4. Because of the maternal imagery I have changed the pronoun from 'he' to 'she'. It cries out for this!

77. Julian of Norwich, *Revelations of Divine Love*, translated by Elizabeth Spearing, Penguin Classics, London 1998, chapter 32.